In Memory of Those Who Are Not With Us Anymore

Based on Russian language novella "Jewish Happiness" that was written in Israel by Lyudmila Levina in 2007 from her conversations with Yehuda Feldman.

First edition 2018 with front and back cover art by Lena Rapoport.

Identifiers: Library of Congress Control Number: 2018909409

ISBN: 978-0-9994768-0-2

Copyright © Ilya Leybovich, 2018.

All Rights Reserved

The author and the publisher do not have control over and do not assume any responsibility for websites and third party content referenced in this book.

DEDICATED TO THE MEMORY OF THE VICTIMS

Do not assume it was easy for me to survive and fight in those terrible conditions. After all, I was all alone ... and I set a goal: not only to survive, but also to help save other people, to save as many of them as possible.

- Yehuda Feldman

DEDICATED TO THE MEMORY OF MY GRANDFATHER

Who spoiled his grandson, always preached the need for a good education, danced at my wedding, and lived to see his first great granddaughter born. He died in the land of his ancestors at the age of 91.

- Ilya Leybovich

CONTENTS

THE STORY BEHIND THIS BOOK 1
INTRODUCTION 2
    1   CHILDHOOD 3
    2   MEETING WITH KRUPSKAYA 17
    3   THE INSTITUTE 20
    4   WAR 25
    5   CAMPS 28
    6   A PROPHETIC DREAM 32
    7   NORWAY 37
    8   RELEASE 42
    9   KOLOMNA AND POCHEP 47
    10   FAREWELL TO KURT! 55
    11   AFTER THE DEMOBILIZATION 57
    12   ISRAEL! 64
    13   IN ISRAEL! 69
    14   MY COUNTRY ISRAEL! 73
APPENDIX 1   SPRING LOVE (LYUBOV YAROVAYA) 77
APPENDIX 2   CHILDREN VANYUSHINA 78
APPENDIX 3   DEMBLINSK FORTRESS 79
APPENDIX 4   IVAN'S FIGHTING IN THE TRENCHES 81
APPENDIX 5   POCHEP MONUMENTS 82
APPENDIX 6   FAMILY WAS DEPORTED 84
APPENDIX 7   DOCTOR'S CASE / ROOTLESS
                            COSMOPOLITANISM 89

THE STORY BEHIND THIS BOOK

For half a century, my grandfather, Yehuda Feldman had been quietly on a mission. Since the 1960's, he sought a person to compile and publish his memoire. I think it was a sense of obligation, to repay those who came to his aid, by keeping the memory of them alive.

My grandfather met Lyudmila Levin through a mutual friend. She was a semi-retired Russian short story writer, who came to his apartment in Israel and took down his life's story. Based on their conversations, Lyudmila wrote a novella of about 90 pages, written in Russian.

It was my grandfather's dream to have his memoire translated into English. This is now the project started. This book and the research around it quickly took a life of its own and turned into a journey of discovery of my Jewish Eastern European roots. My goal for this book is to give those of my generation or later, whose only link to their grandparents is a name of a town or a story of hardship, a deeper understanding of the lives their grandparents lived and choices they made.

Like its Russian counterpart this book is written as a conversation between Yehuda Feldman and Lyudmila Levin. In rewriting the original book, I kept my grandfather's quotes and tone as I remember them while sitting and listening to his amazing experiences.

Some of the references and places referred to by Lyudmila and my grandfather were unfamiliar to me and may be unfamiliar to you. To bring you into this living memory I added maps, photos, sidebars (in gray), and appendixes. I also need to thank all the family, friends, and folks who selflessly gave their time to review and advice in order to make this book happen.

I now invite you along through my grandfather's journey and then to start your own journey of discovery.

- Ilya Leybovich

INTRODUCTION

"Jewish Luck" what bitter irony in those words! Especially since we are talking about a man who spent four years in German captivity, then survived "cleansing" in the Soviet SMERSH "filtration" camp, and despite those twin hells was released unharmed. Who can claim that's not luck? It's pure luck, without any irony.

He told me his life story and I not only wrote down his story but also unwittingly become the co-author of these memoirs, adding my thoughts about what he went through. I not only recorded but also edited the not always correct (in terms of wording and construction of phrases) and rather disjointed biography, making it "coherent". I tried to keep the stories as close to his speech as possible. Those times when he talked about his most tragic and most sentimental moments of his life I transcribed word for word.

The unusual course of his life attracted me to writing this memoir. There are so many tragic stories about the fate of the Jews who survived (or did not survive) those times [Soviet Revolution, Nazi occupation, and Bolshevik Soviet Union]. But how many stories have been told about a happy fate? This is one of them. What helped my hero achieve the incredible: not only to survive, but to get out of that hell unscathed? What was it? A miraculous coincidence? The will to live? Or cautious, intelligent behavior of the man himself? This is for you, the reader, to judge. Here before you is the story of his life.

- Lyudmila Levina

HOW MUCH FURTHER

I
CHILDHOOD

"A person does not live in order to suffer and struggle," with these words my hero began his story. Yehuda Feldman is over 90, alert and active. He is not tall, stocky, and amply proportioned. Not much is left from what many years ago was a lush dark head of hair. His eyes look straight at you from under his thick bushy eyebrows. He speaks slowly, clearly pronouncing each word.

"In 1941, I was twenty-three years old," he began. But I interrupted him, "By the beginning of the war [World War II] you were an adult, a mature man. How did your life begin? Where? Tell me about your family. Let's start from the beginning."

His voice carried as if from long ago.

"My grandfather had a large family; father was my grandfather's seventh son. Grandfather was a teacher at the yeshiva. I only heard about him, he died before I was born. My grandfather lived with his family in **Belarus**.

There, in the Jewish settlement of **Miloslavichi** in December 1918 I was born. In our family, there were five people at that time: father and mother, older sister and brother, and I was the youngest.

Belarus –
a country in Eastern Europe, known for its Stalinist architecture, fortifications and pristine forests.

Miloslavichi –
a village 192 miles East of Minsk. Jews began living there in the mid-19th century. At the turn of the century there were 630 Jews, about half of the population. In 1905, a wave of pogroms struck. Some of the Jews succeeded in halting anti-Jewish violence with the help of peasants from nearby villages.

HOW MUCH FURTHER

Family origin in Belarus, Europe.
Map data ©2017 Google

Father even before the revolution [Communist Revolution], during **World War 1**, was drafted into the army. In Belarus, as well as throughout the country, there was a civil war. It even reached our corner. I was very small then, I do not remember anything. My mother told me that we almost died. A detachment of White Guard [also known as the **Russian White Army**] passed through Miloslavichi. There were so many [soldiers] we lost count of how many. Every commander, entering the town ordered the soldiers to find and shoot the surviving Jews.

They herded to the central plaza dozens of frightened women and among them my mother with me, the youngest (the oldest managed to hide somewhere). A White Guard officer looked at the pitiful group of women and one of them with a child and ordered the soldiers to lower their guns and let them go."

Listening to him I thought, "This was the first time that fate spared my hero. There happened to be a noble officer and gentleman, who considered it shameful to dirty his hands with the blood of defenseless women and children."

World War I – a global war that lasted from July 1914 to November 1918. The Russian government collapsed in March 1917 and a revolution followed in November. By the end of the war, the German Empire, Russian Empire, Austro-Hungarian Empire, and the Ottoman Empire ceased to exist.

Russian White Army – a loose confederation of anti-Communist forces that fought the Bolsheviks.

HOW MUCH FURTHER

He continued his narration: "Soon, our family moved to the city of **Pochep**.

This was no longer a village, but a small town, and not in Belarus but in Russia, in the **Bryansk** region. In the city there were several industrial enterprises, a club, and schools. It was quite picturesque: a wide river flowed through the whole town and a large city garden stretched along the banks. But more importantly, the railroad passed nearby - not the wilderness anymore.

Here the family settled by renting two rooms in the basement of an apartment building. Father returned from the war disabled and was only able to get a job as a watchman. He guarded a large orchard that belonged to a neighboring farm collective. Of course, on the tiny salary of a watchman it would've been simply impossible to feed a family of five and pay the rent.

But already in the mid-twenties [1920's] along with the civil war the terrible era of "war communism" had left and was replaced by **NEP** – "state capitalism". Pochep was

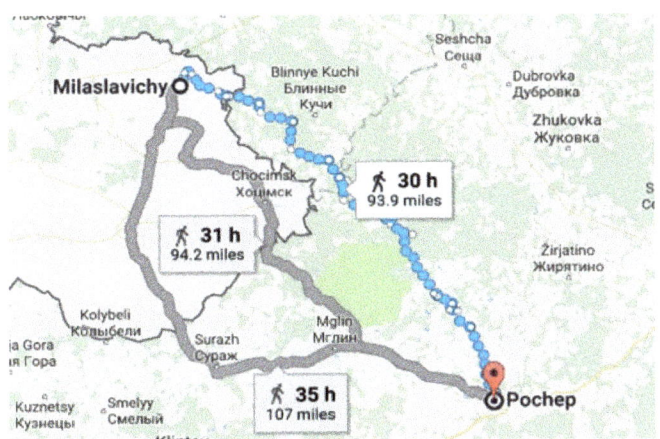

The family moves from Miloslavichi, Belarus to Pochep, Russia.
Map data ©2017 Google

> **Pochep –**
> a small town in the Bryansk region of Russia; 250 miles southwest of Moscow. Jews began to settle in Pochep in the 17th century. In the 1920's, most Pochep Jews were merchants or craftsmen; while engaged in agriculture.
>
> **Bryansk –**
> the capital of the Bryansk region, standing on the banks of the Desna River; about 230 miles West of Moscow. In 1918, the Belarusian Republic claimed Bryansk but the town was taken by Bolshevik forces in 1919.

HOW MUCH FURTHER

a major regional center, located on the border of Belarus and Ukraine. So it was here, on the central square, that a big market gathered every Sunday.

Peasants from neighboring villages traded livestock, poultry, and other goods. The local residents (among them the father, brother, sister, and other relatives of our hero) sold their handmade products as well as goods purchased in other cities. Profits from the trade enabled the family to feed themselves. Thus, although the family was not rich, neither did they know hunger at that time.

"My father was a religious man," he continued. "He wore a long beard and *peyas*." Of course, it was not easy to remain faithful during the Soviet regime. Back then posters hung up everywhere proclaiming: 'Religion is poison, save your children!' But my father thought and acted differently.

Before the synagogue closed, my father took me to worship and taught me prayers. Even when the synagogue closed, he continued to pray every morning and every evening; only at home, alone. At that time, the **CHEKA** [Russian secret police] ran rampant. So, if at least five

NEP – the New Economic Policy was proposed by Vladimir Lenin, who described it as a progression towards "state capitalism". It would include "a free market and capitalism, both subject to state control" while socialized state enterprises were to operate on "a profit basis".

Peyas – the Hebrew word for side locks or side curls. Peyas are worn by some men and boys in the Orthodox Jewish community.

Pochep Market Fair, Early 20th Century.
Attribution: Unknown author; public domain.

HOW MUCH FURTHER

Propaganda poster 1930's 'Religion is poison, save your children!'.
Attribution: Unknown author; public domain.

CHEKA –
the much feared Bolshevik secret police. The CHEKA was formed in the wake of the October Revolution of 1917, established as a small agency to investigate and deal with threats to the new regime. It was to be the "sword and shield of the revolution", defending the Soviet regime by attacking its enemies within.

Shabbat –
is Judaism's day of rest and is the seventh day of the week. It is observed Friday night to Saturday night in remembrance of Biblical creation, in which G-d rested after creating the heavens and the earth in six days.

people who were not relatives gathered at a home, the Chekists regarded it to be a secret organization, the members of which should be immediately arrested.

I first heard the word 'Jew' from my friends in the street when I was six or seven. I asked my father what it meant. In response, my father told me about faith in G-d, and the sanctity of the **Shabbat**. I firmly remember his words: "Keep faith in G-d in your heart and He will help you in a difficult moment." My father often told me about Jewish holidays and traditions. And I remember those stories all my life."

Itzhak Feldman was a role model to his children not only in words but also in his deeds. Once outside the city, he found a package with a large sum of money; it seemed someone had dropped it on the road. He carried his find directly to the police; not giving a second thought to a reward. Back then there wasn't a practice of giving a reward to the finder; even through his family sorely needed the money.

HOW MUCH FURTHER

Here's how he explained the reason behind his action to his children: "You can't build your happiness on someone else's misfortune." Even the local newspaper reported the noble deed of Itzhak Feldman, calling him the most honest man in the city.

"What a blessing to have such a father!" I thought, knowing that later (after leaving Pochep), the boy would join the **Pioneers** [Russian political youth organization] and then the **Komsomol** [Russian youth division of the Communist Party].

Neither the secret police nor the Communist organizations **extinguished the faith in G-d** Yehuda kept in his heart and he remained a Jew. More importantly, he remained an honest and decent person. It helped him a lot during future challenges!

"My mother [her name was Frida] died in childbirth when I was seven years old," continued Yehuda. "Photos of her did not survive. I remember that she was tall, slender, and had large eyes. She was birth mother only to me,

Propaganda poster recruiting children to join Komsomol, 1932. Caption says "Prepare for worthy successors to the Leninist Komsomol".
Attribution: Unknown author; public domain.

Pioneers – an organization for children operated by a Communist Party. Typically children enter into the organization in elementary school and continue until adolescence.

Komsomol – a political youth organization in the Soviet Union. It is sometimes described as the youth division of the Communist Party of the Soviet Union. Although officially independent, it was referred to as "the helper and the reserve of the Communist Party."

the youngest. To the older children she was their aunt, sister of their deceased mother. She did not show favoritism or make a distinction between me and my cousins. Of course, she paid more attention to me, as I was still small. She often took me in her arms and rocked me to sleep, singing lullabies in Yiddish."

He began to sing from memory the ancient lullaby about **Rozhinkes Mit Mandlen** (Raisins with Almonds). "She taught me never to tattletale. And most importantly my parents taught us to love each other and care for each other for the rest of our lives. When she died, my older brother, standing at her grave, gave his word to do everything so that the younger brother would grow up a decent man. He kept his word. But it was not easy; he worked a lot and studied in the evenings (preparing for admission to trade school).

In addition, it was still necessary to help our sister take care of things at home. Yet he found time for me, he talked to me about the books he read, and from him I first heard the name of **Sholem Aleichem, Yitskhok Peretz**, and other Jewish writers. He taught me to love books and people. He also helped me to establish my life in the future. But that is a discussion for later.

After mother's death my sister became the mistress of the house: she cleaned, cooked, and took care of everyone - especially me, the youngest. I got so attached to her, as to a mother, that I could not even fall asleep without her. What a pity that her life was cut so short because of the war!"

Listening to him, I thought: "My hero was lucky with his family!" Here a boy who was orphaned so early received his initial and very valuable lessons for life: honesty, hard work, mutual support, and most importantly - loyalty to his people, its traditions, and culture. Moreover, if you can't

---

Extinguished the faith in G-d – being a Jew in the Soviet Union meant many hated you and open discrimination all around. Your passport and official documents under race listed 'Jew'.

Religion was outlawed; most grew up never knowing about Jewish holidays. The smallest acts of observance, like buying matzo, could result in immediate arrest and subsequent blacklisting from work.

Government policies were in place to limit the number of Jews in universities and receiving promotions. Joining the Communist Party (in effect denouncing Judaism) was one way out.

HOW MUCH FURTHER

Brother Geya and sister Genia.

do something publicly, continue to do so in secret (as his father prayed). But at all times, remain true to yourself.

"What's next?" I asked.

"Soon after mother's death, my sister married and went to live in her husband's house. My brother moved to Moscow and started trade school there. I stayed alone with my disabled father. How to survive? I did not want to stay in Pochep. Moscow beckoned from far away. There my beloved brother, there schools. There I could get not only a basic but a higher education.

I dreamed of becoming a doctor: after all, both my mother and her sister [my aunt] died young. That's why I wanted to prolong a person's life. In Pochep, there wasn't a college nor a hospital, but only three doctors and paramedics who went on house calls.

Rozhinkes Mit Mandlen –
a very popular Yiddish lullaby from the opera "Shulamis" by Abraham Goldfaden. He was the founder of modern Yiddish theatre. Link to the video of the lullaby: www.songsofmypeople.com/rozh

Sholem Aleichem –
one of the founding fathers of modern Yiddish literature. A Jewish humorist, who tapped into East European, spoken-Yiddish idiom, and invented modern Jewish archetypes, myths, and fables.

HOW MUCH FURTHER

So I made up my mind to reach the capital at any cost. One day, late at night, without saying a word to my father, I left the house for the station and got on the first passing train to Moscow. I did not have money for a ticket, so I hid under a bench [in a train cabin], where I spent the night.

Upon waking in the morning, I found a military officer and his wife sitting on the bench under which I hid. My fellow traveler turned out to be a good man: he asked me who I was, where I was going and why. He promised to help me. When we arrived in Moscow he took me to his home, insisted that I take a bath, bought me new clothes, and helped find my brother.

At the time my brother was in the hospital and I lived in the apartment of my accidental fellow-traveler until my brother recovered [from pneumonia]."

"Of course," Yehuda added, "Upon arrival to Moscow, I immediately called my father in Pochep and told him where I was and that I was all right."

Yitskhok Peretz – Yitskhok Leybush Peretz was a Yiddish and Hebrew poet, writer, essayist, dramatist, and cultural figurehead.

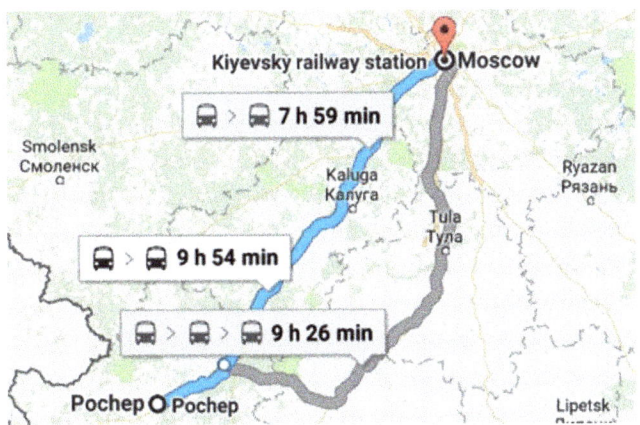

7 years old Yehuda takes a train from Pochep to Moscow.
Map data ©2017 Google

HOW MUCH FURTHER

"Yet another twist in the biography of my hero," I thought. A very risky turn which fortunately ended well. What played a bigger role here? The tenacity of my hero or just luck?

I thought at first, his tenacity: not every seven year old will take a chance to leave home and go on a long and dangerous journey. The boy took a big risk, but nothing ventured, nothing gained. Then, of course, good luck: after all, being thrown off a train for a free ride is not the worst thing that could have been waiting for him. What if his fellow traveler would've turned out to be a clever crook, who could take complete advantage of a weak and defenseless child for the lowest and criminal purposes? Or if, upon arriving in Moscow alone, it turned out that he could not find his brother, but got lost in the huge city, joining the ranks of street urchins? Yes, anything could have happened! Fortunately, it did not happen.

Meanwhile my companion continued: "Finally, my brother was discharged from the hospital and we met. Of course, we were very happy and then we began to think about how and where to find me a place to live and start school. My brother lived in a studio with four other people. For a while, I lived with him, but what's next?

My brother was a member of **Mikhoels'** Jewish organization as well as MONO (Moscow Department of Education). MONO was in charge of all children's housing in the capital and the region. My brother took me to the suburb of Malakhovka near Moscow and arranged for an orphanage which was called *The Jewish Children's Colony*. It was then funded by **JDC** - the international Jewish humanitarian organization.

Both the teachers and the pupils at the time spoke **Yiddish**.

Mikhoels' – Solomon Mikhoels was a Soviet Jewish actor and the artistic director of the Moscow State Jewish Theater. Mikhoels served as the chairman of the Jewish Anti-Fascist Committee during the World War II; a propaganda unit of the secret police that promoted the Soviet war effort among Jews in the West. He was killed by Stalin's secret police on January 13, 1948.

HOW MUCH FURTHER

Yehuda with older brother in Moscow, 1930's.

Even though I wasn't an orphan, my brother, a member of MONO, managed to place me in this colony."

"Once again what luck!" I thought. If his brother was not a member of these organizations, it is unlikely there would be a place for the boy in the colony, and after learning that his father was alive, they would have probably have sent him back to Pochep.

Jewish Children's Colony, 1920's.
Attribution: American Jewish Joint Distribution Committee Archives; NY_43682.

The Jewish Children's Colony – an academic 'experiment' in the era of the transition from the secular schools of the early 20th century to the newly created Soviet system of education after the Revolution.

JDC – an organization whose main goal is to offer aid to the many Jewish populations in Europe plus the Middle East through a network assistance programs.

Yiddish – historical language of the Jews from Central and Eastern Europe. It is a hybrid of Hebrew and medieval German dating to the 12th century. It has its own grammar but is written with Hebrew letters.

HOW MUCH FURTHER

"The orphanage was wonderful," he continued. "The thing was that one American millionaire gave the Soviet government two million dollars for the purchase of grain and asked in return to help Jewish children. **Lenin** replied that the Soviet government would help all children, including Jewish children.

JDC regularly sent money to Russia to support orphanages."

"That's why in Russia in the 1920's it was still possible for Jewish orphanages and the learning of Yiddish to exist," I thought. It was made possible through money from the JDC and an American Jewish millionaire.

Yehuda, as if reading my thoughts, continued. "But three years later the orphanage was taken over by the Ministry of Internal Affairs and the children started to have lessons in Russian."

"Of course," I thought, with the Soviet rule any ethnic institution, let alone a Jewish one, was doomed. Even so, for the prior three years lessons had resounded in Yiddish. The teachers taught the children not only about "Grandpa Lenin" but also about Jewish history - about **Abraham Avinu**, and other heroes. So before **Stalin**'s oppression, a little hometown warmth entered into the souls of these Jewish children.

Lenin –
Vladimir Lenin was a Russian Communist Revolutionary, politician and political theorist. Under his control 1917 - 1924, Russia and then the wider Soviet Union became a one-party communist state governed by the Russian Communist Party.

Abraham Avinu –
Abraham in the Old Testament was the founding father of the Jewish faith.

Stalin –
Joseph Stalin was a Soviet revolutionary and dictator who governed the after Lenin; 1924 to 1953 (his death). His ruthless policies were responsible for mass repressions and millions of deaths through famines and forced labor camps.

Vladimir Lenin, 1920's.
Attribution: German Federal Archive; public domain.

HOW MUCH FURTHER

Joseph Stalin at the Potsdam Conference, 1945.
Attribution: United States Library of Congress; public domain.

A ten-year school program gave pupils a high school education and teachers, working under the **Makarenko** system, sought to develop children's natural abilities and inclinations. To enable this, school offered choir and drama clubs.

"I went to a drama club," recalled Yehuda with a smile. "In the play *Spring Love*, I played the role of Siskin [a small songbird related to the goldfinch], and in the play *Children of Vanyushina*, mostly Vanyushina himself.

Anton Makarenko, 1920's.
Attribution: Unknown author; public domain.

> ***Makarenko –*** Anton Makarenko counted among the world's great educators and one of the founders of Soviet pedagogy. He developed the theory and method of upbringing in self-governing child collectives and introduced the concept of productive labor into the educational system.
>
> ***Spring Love –*** a play set during the Russian Civil War, in a small town, Lyubov is helping the revolutionaries; but her husband, thought dead, has been secretly helping the other side. More in Appendix 1.

HOW MUCH FURTHER

Writers came to visit the orphanage. I remember the arrival of the Jewish poet **Peretz Markish**. He read his poems, and after meeting him, I fell in love with literature even more. The orphanage had a good library. I read books by Sholom Aleichem and other Jewish writers. Thus ended my childhood and came the time of my adolescence," recounted my hero.

"It wasn't too bad," I thought.

Difficulties forged the boy's character. He grew up early and thought about life. His family filled his soul with warmth, instilled faith in G-d in his heart, and pride in his people. He was educated among Jewish children and was not aware of anti-Semitism, which could leave painful wounds in a child's vulnerable soul. It was time to embark on life's adventure. What would happen next?

Peretz Markish, 1920's.
Attribution: Unknown author; public domain.

Children of Vanyushina – a play showing the collapse of a merchant's family. The family is ruled by greed. The father is a stranger to his children reaping the fruits of his omissions. More in Appendix 2.

Peretz Markish – a Soviet/Russian Jewish poet and playwright who wrote mainly in Yiddish. In the 1920's he published a number of optimistic poems glorifying the communist regime. He was awarded the Order of Lenin in 1939 and joined the Communist party in 1942.

Under Stalin, in 1949 Markish was accused of being a "Jewish nationalist", and arrested. He was shot with other Jewish writers during the Night of the Murdered Poets in 1952.

II
MEETING WITH KRUPSKAYA

Yehuda continued, "Most of all I was fascinated by medicine. I firmly decided after graduation to apply to a medical institute.

In 1935, while I was attending 9th grade, an event transpired that set the path for the rest of my life. *Nadezhda Krupskaya* [widow of Vladimir Lenin] came to visit our colony.

At the orphanage I was the "kultorgom" [cultural event planner] and Krupskaya wanted to meet me.

She said to me: "When you finish the 10th year, come, and I will send you to study, where you want." She gave me the address of the People's Commissariat for Education (now called the Ministry of Education). At the time Lenin's widow was the deputy of the People's Commissar of Education.

Nadezhda Krupskaya near Moscow, Russia, 1936.
Attribution: State Museum of Political History of Russia; public domain.

Nadezhda Krupskaya – born to an upper class but impoverished family. She became a Russian Bolshevik revolutionary, politician, and the wife of Vladimir Lenin from 1898 until his death in 1924. She served as the Soviet Union's Deputy Minister of Education from 1929 until her death in 1939.

HOW MUCH FURTHER

On September 8, 1936, when I finished the ten-year program, I came into the office of N.K. Krupskaya. She stood me in front of a map of the country's universities and invited me to choose a city where I would like to study. My first choice was **Kiev** and I said that I wanted to live and study there; she recommended the Second Medical University. On September 13th, I was already in Kiev and handing the director of the institute a letter from Krupskaya, was immediately taken to the auditorium and admitted without the entrance exams."

Once again, Yehuda was lucky. Not everyone at that time could so easily and freely gain access to higher education. Of course, circumstances helped: children from poor families, especially from orphanages, were admitted to universities first and without restrictions. Then there was a letter of recommendation from Krupskaya. Such patronage!

However, in order to deserve this, it was necessary to gain recognition among his comrades, to become a leader in school, and thus attract the attention of Krupskaya. Plus, he chose a hardworking and humanitarian profession like

Kiev – the capital and largest city of Ukraine. Starting in the late 1920's the city turned from a center of commerce and religion into a major industrial, technological, and scientific center. In 1934 Kiev became the capital of Soviet Ukraine. The city boomed again during the years of the Soviet industrialization (1932–1933) as its population grew rapidly and many industrial giants were created, some of which exist to this day.

Kiev Ukraine, 2010's.
Attribution: Max Pixel; public domain.

HOW MUCH FURTHER

medicine - a profession that would later save his life.

But in order to achieve this profession, my hero faced a difficult and relentless curriculum.

III
THE INSTITUTE

"The first semester passed, and I received a stipend from the Presidium of the Supreme Soviet of the USSR in the amount of 180 rubles, which was a lot of money at the time. From then until the very end of the institute, every three months I received such a financial allowance, plus a scholarship, free meals in the cafeteria, and free accommodation in the dorms. Thanks to this I was considered a 'wealthy student' compared to the rest of my friends in the dorm."

He dove head first into his studies: he bought books, attended lectures by professors and associate professors.

"I remember the first 'anatomist' (morgue) visit at a city hospital. At first it was scary to see the corpses which under the scalpel in front of your eyes turned into separate fragments and organs of the human body. But if you can't take control of yourself you will never be a doctor! I pulled myself together and got accustomed to it."

It was fortunate that from the beginning Yehuda was able to take advantage of the chances fate had given him. "Use the present for a brighter future" was an aphorism that I had written somewhere in my youth and which often comes to mind now. But surely an eighteen year old man living in a large and beautiful city wanted to forget his text books at least for a while? At least sometimes leave behind the studying and the dissecting, to enjoy beauty, youth, and love?

HOW MUCH FURTHER

The narration continued, as if answering my questions: "The first two years were nonstop studying. But after all, youth takes its own! I lived in a beautiful old city; there were places to go and things to see. And all around there were so many beautiful girls! And, of course, there were the romances.

I remember one date, just before the end of the Institute. Her name was Ledecka. She loved movies and entertainment - but I had to study! It was difficult to carve out time to go to the theater with Lidochka. In Kiev, at the time, before the war, there was a Jewish theater. Knowing that she was from a poor family I often helped her with money."

A cautious attitude toward money and the desire to help others: those were the priceless qualities that helped my hero, especially in future trials. Although young, he was very goal-oriented.

Another would have squandered the money or simply spent it on himself, so I thought listening to him.

"Tell me about the people living with you in the dorm," I asked. He readily said: "There were four people in the

Captain of Medical Service, Yehuda Feldman, May 1941.

HOW MUCH FURTHER

room. We attended lectures together, studied at home, and rested. We lived amicably. One of my comrades, Victor Chekanov, later saved my life; but more about that later.

When I was in my third year, I was sent to the Kiev Military Medical School. There we trained to become military doctors and upon completion became commissioned officers. The training took place once a week and the remaining days I studied at the [Kiev Second] Institute. It was prestigious to study at the military medical school: after all we were training to become military doctors.

In 1941 each cadet was measured, and tailor fitted into his uniform and boots. How nice it was to walk through the streets of Kiev in a brand new uniform, saluting the infantry officers! We differed from them only in that we were not supposed to carry firearms.

In May 1941, I received a diploma from the medical institute and the rank of Captain of Medical Service from the Kiev Military Medical School; our 7th group was on the track of Military Medical Academy."

"Tell me, in Kiev before the war didn't you sense anti-Semitism? After all, in the medical institute Ukrainians, Russians, and students of other nationalities studied together. Were there any Jews besides you?" I asked.

"In our institute there were about ten Jewish students. I swear, having lived 51 years in the USSR (before leaving for Israel), I felt no anti-Semitism at all! Once, before the war, when Leda and I went on a tram to meet her parents, a young man came to us and said, 'there sits *a zhid*.' Then one of the other passengers approached the youth and threw him out of the still moving tram."

A zhid – a derogatory slang term for a Jewish person.

Anti-Semitic pressure was building across Eastern Europe for centuries. In 1903 an anti-Semitic fabricated book called "The Protocols of the Elders of Zion" was published in Russia and translated into many languages. Some of its publishers claimed it to be the minutes of a late 19th-century meeting where Jewish leaders discussed their goal of global Jewish domination. It was a complete lie and fabrication.

HOW MUCH FURTHER

So, then, anti-Semitism existed before the war, but it was not allowed to flourish and got nipped in the bud. The locals were vigilant to curb anti-Semitism and not get infected with this dangerous disease. But more importantly the powers that were not only didn't support anti-Semitic sentiments at the time but strongly suppressed it in every way, including through legislation. Is that right?" I asked.

"Of course. Back then you could get sent to the slammer for uttering the word '*zhid*'. These days very few people know that it was by Lenin's initiative that **L. D. Trotsky** was appointed People's Commissar [now Minister of Defense]. When Trotsky protested: 'Vladimir Ilyich [Lenin], but after all I am a Jew' - Lenin angrily exclaimed: 'Damn it! For what did we have a revolution!'"

Yehuda added that Lenin's speeches were once recorded on vinyl records. In an early speech, he stated that the Bolshevik revolution once and for all put an end to anti-Semitism.

So I thought, "That is how the Bolsheviks always dealt with the uncomfortable facts in their history: they simply expunged them. Well, how could they preserve such statements by Lenin, when anti-Semitism in the USSR became federal policy in the 1950's!"

"So, in May 1941, a month before the start of the war [World War II], you received a medical degree and a military commission. Where were you posted? And what happened next?" I asked. He continued his story.

> ***L. D. Trotsky*** – a Marxist revolutionary and theorist - a Soviet politician who engineered the transfer of all political power to the Soviets with the October Revolution of 1917 and the founding leader of the Red Army.

HOW MUCH FURTHER

L. D. Trotsky, 1929.
Attribution: Bundesarchiv, Bild 183-R15068 / CC-BY-SA 3.0; public domain.

HOW MUCH FURTHER

IV
WAR

"On June 15, 1941, I arrived in the territory of Western Belarus in the city of **Brest-Litovsk**. It was only one week before the start of the war, but no one knew about the imminent disaster. I was glad to observe the peaceful life of the people, but the joy did not last long. On June 25, 1941, I lived through the terrible minutes when planes with black crosses first appeared in the sky. I saw a horrible scene: a mother with a nursing baby just sat down to feed the child and in that moment a German plane over them dropped a bomb. I, as a physician, was accustomed to the sight of blood and corpses, but only in a hospital and in the morgue. But here, right on the street I was trembling!"

Even now, talking about it, he could not conceal his trepidation. Then, a little calmer, he continued: "I was assigned to a tank regiment, which was in **Kobryn**. There I learned that the war had already begun. I immediately joined the work: I actively participated in the creation of an evacuation hospital. The first wounded soon came.

After some time, the regiment commander came to me and ordered to prepare for the evacuation of the wounded and warned me not to take any actions by myself. The evacuation was expected in half an hour. But half an hour later instead of the Soviet soldiers, a German officer

> *Brest-Litovsk* – a city in Belarus at the border with Poland. On June 22, 1941, the city was attacked by Germany on the first day of the anti-Soviet Operation Barbarossa. Abandoned by the Soviet army, nearly all its defenders perished.

HOW MUCH FURTHER

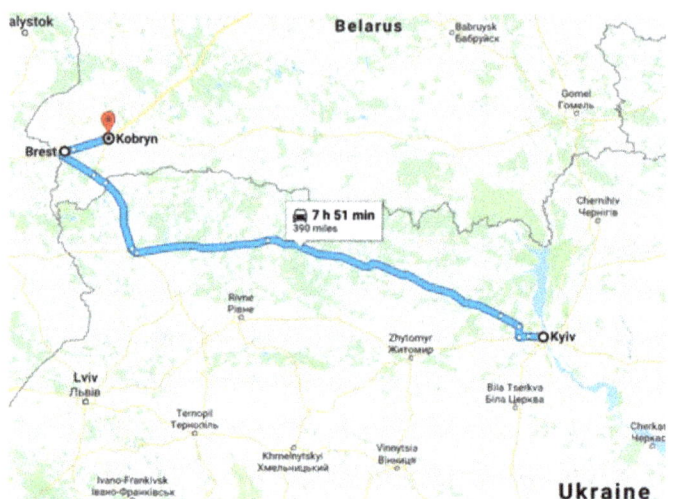

After graduation in Kiev to assignment in Brest-Litovsk and deployment in Kobryn.
Map data ©2018 Google

Kobryn – a city in the Brest Region of Belarus. Between 1939 and 1941 the town was occupied by the Soviet Union, then from 23 June 1941 to 20 July 1944 by Nazi Germany.

came to me with two soldiers: the city was already occupied Germans. I told the German officer that this is a military hospital. The German officer said what he recently heard from the Russian commander, that a car will soon be sent to evacuate the wounded. Indeed, after 15 minutes a car was sent and the wounded were evacuated to Brest-Litovsk.

My friend and roommate from the institute, Victor Chekanov, worked with me in the hospital. As soon as we fell into German captivity, he immediately came and asked me, 'What did you do with your documents in which your last name is Feldman?' I replied that I destroyed all my documents. He said, 'You did the right thing: if the Germans find out that you are a Jew, you would be immediately shot. From now on you will carry my surname: Chekanov [his first name was disguised as well]. We'll say that we are family and that your documents are lost.' So I did. Thank you, my friend, otherwise I would have perished."

HOW MUCH FURTHER

Russian tanks going to the front. T-34 Tanks, 1942.
Attribution: RIA Novosti archive, image #1274 / RIA Novosti / CC-BY-SA 3.0.

Listening to him I thought: "There is nothing bad without something good in it." My hero did not have to see combat, that is, to take part in the fighting. It was good that he was met by a German officer who, judging by his actions, was not a Nazi but simply served in the **Wehrmacht**. For him a wounded soldier was no longer an enemy but a person in need of help. And a military doctor was just a doctor.

There is a Russian proverb, "Do not keep a hundred rubles [Russian currency] but keep a hundred friends." True to the proverb, a friend in misfortune at once came to Yehuda's aid and saved him from certain death.

Yehuda continued, "The next day I was summoned to the hospital deputy chief (he was from the **Volga Germans**) who said to me: 'Doctor, I must send you to the general camp, because soon the **Gestapo** will arrive here to identify the Communists and the Jews.'"

Wehrmacht – the unified armed forces of Nazi Germany from 1935 to 1946. It consisted of the Heer (army), the Kriegsmarine (navy) and the Luftwaffe (air force).

Volga Germans – ethnic Germans who colonized and historically lived along the River Volga in the region of southeastern European Russia.

Gestapo – the secret police of Nazi Germany and German occupied Europe. Created in 1933 the Gestapo later played a key role in the Nazi plan to exterminate the Jews of Europe by coordinating the concentration camp activity.

V
CAMPS

"So I ended up in a huge camp which was located in *Biala Podlaska* [Poland]. This camp occupied a territory of around two kilometers long by half a kilometer wide. In this area, packed closely together, were about five hundred thousand people."

"And that's just in one camp!" I thought. What a terrible scale this disaster had taken on a national scale and how difficult it was to survive in this meat grinder!

Biala Podlaska – in 1621, 30 Jewish families were granted rights of residence in Biała Podlaska. In Oct 1939 the Soviets handed the town to the Germans. Although not a closed ghetto, by 1940 there were 8,400 Jews crammed into the Jewish Quarter and a typhus epidemic broke due to the appalling sanitary conditions causing many fatalities. In 1942 some 10,800 Jews from around Biała Podlaska were killed.

Biala Podlaska Ghetto liquidation action conducted in 1942.
Attribution: Unknown author; public domain.

HOW MUCH FURTHER

"A terrible rumor spread through the camp," Yehuda echoed my thoughts. "Here appeared a Ukrainian by the name of **Demjanjuk**. G-d forbid, if he meets a Jew: he will tear him to pieces instantly. I think you'll understand how scared I was."

"Did you meet with this two-legged beast?" I asked.

"No, G-d spared me." Yehuda replied.

"How on this small patch of land did my hero manage to outmaneuver certain death?" I thought.

Yehuda continued: "Two days later, a German officer arrived at the camp and announced: 'If there are doctors, come out. Imposters will be shot on the spot.' I came out and was sent back to the hospital at Brest-Litovsk."

"So like the first time, his profession saved him. If he was not a doctor and remained at that camp longer than two days, he would have surely not missed a run-in with Demjanjuk!" I thought. Involuntarily I remembered lines from a story by **Mikhail Sholokhov, The Fate of Man**: "and again, death has passed by, only a chill from it drawn" was recited by the main protagonist who also was a prisoner of war of a Nazi concentration camp.

Demjanjuk – John Demjanjuk was a retired Ukrainian-American, a former soldier in the Soviet Red Army, and a POW during the Second World War.

He was convicted in 2011 as an accessory to the murder of 28,060 Jews while acting as a guard at an extermination camp in occupied Poland.

John Demjanjuk, photo from a suspected forged Nazi ID card, 1940's.
Attribution: Unknown author; public domain.

HOW MUCH FURTHER

He continued: "From June to September, I was in that hospital. And in September, I was transferred to ***Demblinsk [Dęblin] Fortress***. This fortress in Poland was built by ***Catherine II*** for her soldiers. In this fortress I saw real hell: I saw how they destroyed healthy people by poisoning them."

"Doubtlessly using them as guinea pigs, testing the effect of drugs and poisons," I guessed.

The conversation continued: "There were about ten thousand prisoners of war here: French, Polish, and Russian. The Jews were no longer there: they were identified and destroyed even earlier."

> ***Mikhail Sholokhov, The Fate of Man*** –
> the story of a man whose life was ruthlessly crippled by World War II. His wife and daughters were killed during the bombing of his village, he spent some time as a prisoner, and his only son was killed in action only a few days before the victory.
>
> ***Demblinsk [Dęblin] Fortress*** –
> from autumn of 1941 until February 1944 the fortress operated as German Stalag 307, through which passed about 150,000 Soviet prisoners of war. More than half of them died from hunger, cold, and disease. More in Appendix 3.

Demblinsk Fortress where between 1941 and 1942 up to 500 people were killed per day.
Attribution: National Heritage Board of Poland; public domain.

HOW MUCH FURTHER

Yehuda could have been destroyed in Kobryn after the Gestapo arrived. How fortunate that the deputy head of the hospital, a German from the Volga region, transferred Yehuda in time to the general camp. Then Dęblin, that hell was not for the Jews: the Nazis apparently believed that all the Jews had already been exterminated. Only death awaited the Jews.

My companion confirmed my suspicions: "I was the only Jew there and survived only because the Germans did not know about this: first, I did not look like a Jew and secondly, as I said, I did not carry my last name but the last name of my friend Chekanov. We were together until the end of the war."

> *Catherine II* – also known as Catherine the Great (1729 – 1796), was the most renowned and the longest ruling female Empress of Russia. Her rule is often considered the Golden Age of the Russian Empire.

VI
A PROPHETIC DREAM

"This is how I lived until the spring of 1942," continued Yehuda. "We four doctors of prisoners of war were under the command of a German doctor. Seeing the terrible pictures of the mass destruction of people, we decided to go for the sake of their salvation into a deathly risky venture: we decided to declare to the German camp command that a typhus epidemic had begun in the fortress. We demanded the immediate withdrawal of the German guards from the fortress.

The fascists left the fortress, but the executions of the prisoners of war did not stop. The Germans came up with a way to remain outside the fortress and to shoot the prisoners point-blank from above, turning their victims into living targets like in a shooting gallery. An order was given that daily from 9 AM to 12 PM the prisoners would be led out to the central square of the fortress and from above the German officers practiced shooting live people. Isn't this a shooting gallery? And every day a hundred people were shot.

I said that I was the only Jew there but that is not exactly true. I had a friend in the camp, a Jew, and of course his life was in greater danger than the lives of other prisoners who were not Jewish. I decided to save him. He was still a young man, about thirty years old. His name was Moses. He was from **Kharkov** and very tall. I said to him: 'If you want to survive in this hell stay close to us (me and the three other doctors). Do not leave us to go anywhere and if we survive, you'll survive too.'"

HOW MUCH FURTHER

"What were the duties of the prisoner doctors in this death camp, where the main goal was to exterminate as many people as possible? Was there really a need for a doctor? Why where you kept there?" I asked.

"I had a terrible responsibility," he replied. "It was my duty to go out at twelve noon every day to the place of execution of the prisoners (the camp shooting gallery), and check whether all the victims were dead."

"That is, to check the shooting accuracy of these monsters," I thought.

Yehuda continued, "Moses always went with me but one day he was not there. Then I learned that being starved, like all prisoners, he tried to get extra food. He went into the kitchen and said he was a barber (barbers were allotted an additional ration). But the cooks working in the cafeteria were Ukrainians, who immediately saw that it was a Jew, and right away reported this to their German commander.

19th-century view of Kharkiv with the Assumption Cathedral.
Attribution: www.goodfreephotos.com; public domain.

Kharkov – the second largest city in Ukraine. During World War II the city was captured by the Nazis in October 1941. There was a Red Army offensive that failed to capture the city in May 1942. The Jewish population of Kharkov, who prided themselves on having the second largest synagogue in Europe, suffered greatly. Between December 1941 and January 1942, an estimated 30,000 people were killed and buried in a mass grave by the Germans in a ravine outside of town named Drobytsky Yar.

HOW MUCH FURTHER

The commander shot Moses on the spot."

"So much for the absence of anti-Semitism in the USSR!" I thought. As if the Ukrainian cooks, who voluntarily betrayed a Jew to the Germans, did not live in the USSR before the war, but descended to the camp from the moon.

Yehuda continued, "Then one night, my thoughts turned to G-d with the words, 'G-d take my soul, so that I will no longer suffer! I can no longer endure this horror.' The next day, one of the prisoners turned to me with a request: 'Doctor! If you stay alive and you have to stay alive - tell of how we died in this hell!'"

"That's the answer from the Most High to your request for him to take your soul," I said. "Through this prisoner as if He says: 'You must live to tell about what you have seen and I will help you to do that.'"

The conversation continued: "About a week passed since that night, when I turned to G-d with a request to relieve me from this terror even at the cost of my life. I had a dream. I'm flying high in the sky. Flying fast and high and all around me are solid clouds; I do not see anything. I think: 'Where am I flying? Where?'

Suddenly, sparks flash in the pitch darkness: they are stars! They drew me to them. I'm starting to go down and see before me a great synagogue. She gleams with gold and silver. And then I am on the ground. The gates open. I'm going. My G-d! I see my father. He is sitting next to some old man. An old man dressed in white, as if for **Yom Kippur**.

> **Yom Kippur** – it is one the most important holiday of the Jewish year. The name "Yom Kippur" means "Day of Atonement." Many Jews, who do not observe any other Jewish custom, will fast, refrain from work, and attend synagogue services on this day.

HOW MUCH FURTHER

My father says, 'My son! Come to me! We are waiting for you. Next to me is your grandfather!' The old man, whom father called my grandfather, gets up, takes me by the hand, and we go to a place of the shrine where the *Torah* stands.

My grandfather turns to G-d saying, 'Help my grandson to go on living! Get him out of the hell where he is now.' Grandfather disappears and I hear my father's voice: 'My son! I know it's hard for you now. But remember that your grandfather gave you a mandate.

First, you will be freed from captivity and nothing will threaten your life further. Second, remember, you will get out alive and immediately go home. For now, it's too early for you to go to Israel. When the time comes, your life's path itself will lead you to Israel and there will begin your new life.'

When I awoke, I heard the shots again, the cries of the dying - again the terrible camp life returned. 'Lord!? Is what I've seen just a dream?' But what I had been promised in the dream began to come true; I began to feel a little safer than before. What happened? When the Germans came to identify Communists and Jews, they passed me, as if oblivious of me."

"Was there more to this dream?" I wondered. Subconscious thoughts of a prisoner who awaited death every minute? Or was this dream a sign from On-High? You could think of it as either one. Passing by as if not noticing? He became familiar, long known, and besides a doctor, who can be sent to "typhoid" infected prisoners while you stay safe. The father is next to his grandfather? The father who at that time was already dead. Return to Israel? A state with

Torah – the central reference of Judaism. It is transcribed as the five books of the Old Testament.

that name did not exist in the world at that time; it was a ***British Mandate for Palestine***. But in any case the dream supported the weakening resolve of a captive and instilled in him the belief of eventual liberation.

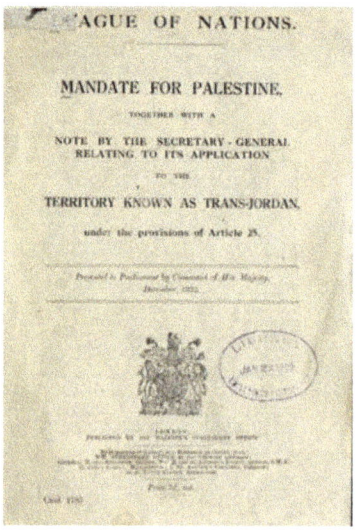

British Command Paper 1785, containing the Mandate for Palestine and the Transjordan memorandum, Dec 1922.
Attribution: Her Majesty's Stationery Office; public domain.

British Mandate for Palestine – a League of Nations mandate for non-self-governing territories that had formerly constituted the Ottoman Empire. The objective was to administer parts of the defunct Ottoman Empire, "until such time as they are able to stand alone".

The Mandate terminated on 14 May 1948. On the last day of the Mandate, the creation of the State of Israel was proclaimed.

VII
NORWAY

"In April 1942, two hundred and fifty prisoners were selected, including me as a doctor, and sent under guard by rail car to Norway, Yehuda said. "On the way to Norway **we were bombarded** by British ships but thank G-d, we made it safely. I was the only doctor among those people. The name of the Norwegian city, where we were, was called **Åndalsnes**.

There I organized a hospital for the 250 port workers.

At that time, it was very difficult to procure medicines and dressings. There was a good private pharmacy in this city. I made a connection with the pharmacist; his name was Miklenbuus. He gave an order to give me free dressings. I

Åndalsnes, 1948.
Attribution: Anders Beer Wilse; public domain.

We were bombarded – Yehuda said this trip was part train and part forced march. While marched the prisoners would come under bombardment and drop flat to the ground. At one particularly heavy bombardment mortar shells were destroying soldiers around the group. One shell landed right between Yehuda's legs and did not go off.

Yehuda attributed this to his grandfather's blessing.

HOW MUCH FURTHER

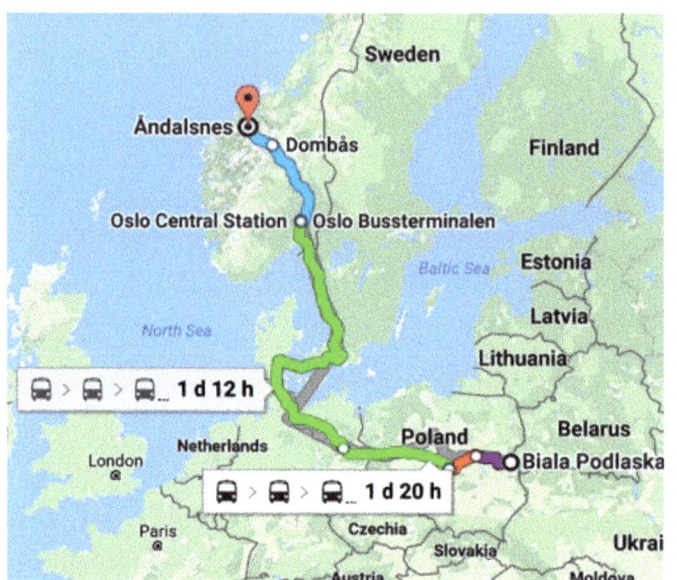

Prisoners taken from Biala Podlaska Poland to work in port city of Åndalsnes Norway.
Map data ©2017 Google

could thus save a lot of patients, as the Germans did not give us anything. The hospital was located in a small room. I attended the sick and if necessary gave them a release from work.

There was an underground anti-fascist organization operating in Norway which disseminated leaflets in German warning that for the killing of a single prisoner ten Germans will be annihilated. Here we no longer feared for our lives, like we did in Dęblin, where it was a living hell."

"Again, a happy turn in the fate of prisoners of Nazi concentration camps," I thought. From the horror of Dęblin where all prisoners sooner or later would be destroyed Yehuda ends up in the *relatively calm* and safe Norway. Here the prisoners could no longer fear for their lives. Here he was able to directly engage in his medical

Åndalsnes – town in Norway located at the mouth of the Rauma river.

Relatively calm – according to Yehuda the city of Åndalsnes was still not safe for Jews. The Gestapo would regularly search for Jews and resistance fighters. Being the only doctors for miles around the hospital workers used to hide him behind large rolls of medical dressings from the Nazis.

The hospital workers were helping a man who saved many lives, and not because they suspected he was a Jew. Not that a Nazi commander needed any justification to kill a Russian prisoner of war.

work: to heal and save people and not check for pulses of shot prisoners, ascertaining their death.

"Do not assume it was easy for me to survive and fight in these terrible conditions," continued Yehuda. "After all, I was all alone; no Jews nearby. I set a goal: not only to survive, but also to help save other people, to save as many of them as possible.

Of course, I can't recount these events without gratitude to our Norwegian helpers. Most of all the pharmacist Renlyard Miklenbuus and his assistant Anna Berglyang. They gave everything they could to treat my patients, including medicines and dressings.

There is one person I want to mention particularly: Kurt, a German guard who accompanied me to the pharmacy and back. He and Miklenbuus knew each other and spoke German. Kurt called us, the Russian prisoners, 'my friends'. We talked a lot with him. He told me: 'When I was leaving for the frontline, my mother told me: Do not kill anyone and do not do evil to people; do only good.'

Kurt told me that before the war he was a teacher and he remembered that his father, at the beginning of the war, foresaw that Germany would be defeated in the war with Russia. It being Russia, a huge country, is much easier to enter than to get out of it. He, like Kurt's mother, urged her son to be kind to people and said they would wait for his return."

"My hero was lucky to find good people," I thought. Everywhere were guardian angels to help him. How else could he survive and carry out his doctor's duties?

HOW MUCH FURTHER

Vyacheslav Molotov. Minister of Foreign Affairs of the USSR, 1930's.
Attribution: Dutch National Archives, The Hague, Fotocollectie AlgemeenNederlands Persbureau (ANEFO), 1945-1989.

Vyacheslav Molotov – a Soviet politician and diplomat, an Old Bolshevik, and a leading figure in the Soviet government from the 1920's. He was a principal architect of the Nazi – Soviet nonaggression pact of 1939 (Molotov–Ribbentrop Pact), which included a secret protocol that called for the invasion of Poland and the partition of its territory between Nazi Germany and the Soviet Union.

"Then one day," continued my companion, "Kurt brought me a newspaper in German, which published a speech by ***Vyacheslav Molotov***, the Minister of Foreign Affairs of the USSR, charging Nazi Germany with mass extermination of Jews. Soon two men in civilian clothes came to me and asked me what I thought about it. I said nothing."

"Probably, the Gestapo; he did the right thing!" I thought. What was the point of looking for trouble? What would it have achieved? Who would have heard him except for the fascists? The prisoners would have lost their only doctor. So, it wasn't yet time to yell of what he saw at the top of his voice.

Yehuda continued his story: "Once I was summoned by a German doctor who told me he's sending me to 'a place where there isn't a doctor yet.' I [soon] found myself in a quiet mountainous place. It was a resort for German officers."

"What, in a resort for German officers there wasn't a doctor? And you treated these officers?" I asked.

HOW MUCH FURTHER

"No, of course not. I was to treat the ten servants, who were actually prisoners." Yehuda explained. "I met a girl there, who lived not far from the resort. Her name was Anna. She was pretty and I was young: I was twenty-three years old. This girl fell in love with me and told me so. But I told her that now was not the time to think of love: there is a war and I am a prisoner. She looked at me, said nothing, and silently went to her house, which stood on the mountain and shone in the rays of the sun."

This is how unexpectedly and poetically he finished this story about his unrequited love and suddenly fell silent. "*Oh, war, you deviant, what have you done!*" I remembered the verses from the song *by Bulat Okudzhava*.

Oh, war, you deviant, what have you done! – a Russian song commemorating people's hardships during WW II. The full song can be found on YouTube: www.youtube.com/watch?v=RTwqh1Qqucg

Bulat Okudzhava – a Soviet poet, writer, and singer-songwriter. He was a founder of the Soviet genre called "author song" or "guitar song", and wrote about 200 songs.

Bulat Okudzhava at Palace of the Republic, Berlin, Germany, 1976.
Attribution: Bundesarchiv, Bild 183-R1202-0019 / Reiche, Hartmut / CC-BY-SA 3.0.

IIX
RELEASE

After a short pause Yehuda continued: "Three years passed and on May 9th we were lined up and told, 'You are free.'"

"Who said that? The Germans?" I asked.

"No. They had already left. So I looked at the house where my Anna lived, my unfulfilled love. But what could I tell her?

Neither she nor her parents knew that I was a Jew and that my way lay with the land of my ancestors. Would she go with me? Was my love for her really that strong? Was it an infatuation? Was it worth embarrassing and deceiving a young soul? I sighed and walked past."

Sverre Knutsen, newly instated chief of police and prosecuting authority in Hamar, Norway, addresses Soviet prisoners of war as they are liberated from a camp near Hamar, May 1945.
Attribution: Photography by Eyolf Knutsen; public domain.

HOW MUCH FURTHER

"Very noble," I thought. For a passing romance there are other women, and there are many, given that the war broke so many families and so many young widows dream of happiness, even if it's short and fleeting!

Yehuda continued: "I took a train and arrived in the capital of Norway, Oslo. For the first time after liberation from captivity, wandering through this beautiful city, I felt what a peaceful life is. I came to the Soviet consulate and there gave my real name. On the appointed day, I arrived at the appointed place and saw many former prisoners. We were loaded into wagons and taken to Sweden and from there by steamship to Leningrad [St. Petersburg USSR].

We were put in a **SMERSH filtration camp** for MIA in **Dubrovka**. There I saw many of the same prisoners who were with me in the camp in 1941. And I was sure that none of them would say a bad word about me.

The next morning I was called by a commissioner. He asked where my parents were. I replied that before the war, my father lived in Pochep, Bryansk Region, and that I did not know where he was now. Then the commissioner asked me about the place of service in the Red Army. I named the

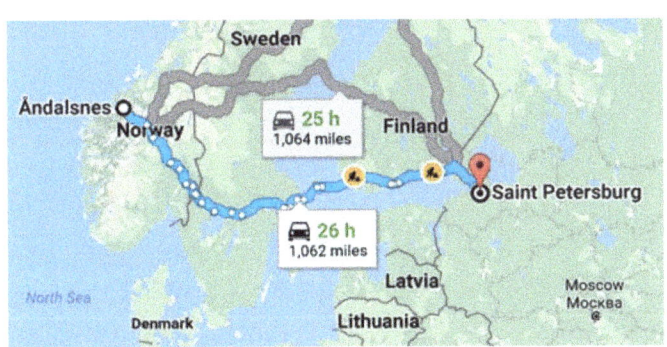

Yehuda's trip from being freed to repatriation by Russia.
Map data ©2017 Google

SMERSH filtration camp – on May 11, 1945, two days after the German surrender, Stalin issued a decree establishing 74 staging camps for former prisoners of war liberated in what became Soviet-occupied eastern Europe. These camps were used to detain liberated Red Army POWs until SMERSH could vet them ("filter" was the official term) for anti-Communist or anti-Russian views, and for other suspect categories of political or social "crimes".

About 1.8 million returning POWs were processed in SMERSH "filtration camps"). The death rate was around 9%.

HOW MUCH FURTHER

Soviet soldiers returning from German captivity now needed to prove that they were not traitors to the Motherland, 1944-1945.
Attribution: Author unknown; public domain.

Dubrovka – a town near Leningrad, Russia.

number of my unit (number 9688), the tank regiment, that was stationed in Kobryn.

Another question I was asked was how I, a Jew, was able to survive and live through four years in German captivity. I replied that you can ask any of the former prisoners with whom I was together in the German camp; they are here in the filtration camp. They, back then in German captivity, saved me. To all questions of the Germans, whether there are Jews among the prisoners, no one betrayed me.

However, not all Russians knew me by my Jewish name: most thought I was Russian. But the few who knew that I was Jewish could have given me up at any time, but did not.

Then the commissioner began to call witnesses. The first of them told me later how he responded to the question of whether he knew that I was Jewish. He replied that he knew, but did not want to inform on me because I was the only doctor among the prisoners and could help them."

HOW MUCH FURTHER

"This is how even earlier, before being sent to Dęblin, his chosen profession saved him," I thought.

"I found out later," he continued "that forty witnesses were interrogated in my case. Everyone said the same thing."

"There, certainly, was a hand of the Most High," I thought. Of the forty respondents no scoundrel and traitor! Unfortunately not everyone was so fortunate. But, probably, it was a matter of personal qualities of a man, his character.

After a short pause, Yehuda confirmed my guess. "For four years I was in captivity and every minute awaited death. I survived, and why? I did not poke my nose where it did not belong and knew my medical business. People around did not know that I was a Jew, and those who knew did not sell my life for a pack of tobacco."

"These same people in concert answered the commissioner's questions without leaving the slightest shadow on the biography of a fellow Jew!" I thought. A deep bow to them for that! What a pity that their names did not survive! These are real righteous people! How many of them had vanished in Stalin's camps with the stigma of traitors to the Motherland!

My companion continued: "Then the commissioner called me and said that the Soviet authorities no longer have any issues with me and I am free. He asked me where I wanted to go. I said that the first place I wanted to go to was **Kolomna**, where lived the mother of my friend Victor Chekanov who saved my life by giving me his surname. I described in detail about how it happened and said that my friend is now here, in the same camp, but was not yet released, as I am, and his mother does not know anything about it. The commissioner wrote down my story and

Kolomna – an ancient city about 71 miles (by rail) southeast of Moscow dating back to 1177.

promised to convey through the chain of command all he heard from me about my friend, and to do everything possible for him to be released soon."

The Cathedral Square, Old Town of Kolomna, Russia, 2014.
Attribution: A.Savin; public domain.

HOW MUCH FURTHER

IX
KOLOMNA AND POCHEP

"So now I'm finally free. I am Yehuda Feldman again. All my documents are restored, including my former military rank of captain of medical service. I warmly said goodbye to Victor, who gave me a letter to his mother. Now here I am in Kolomna, which is not far from Leningrad. The mother of my friend read the letter from her son and wept bitterly. I reassured her as I could."

My companion fell silent, lost in his thoughts. I interrupted the uncomfortable pause with a question: "Do you know anything about the eventual fate of your friend?" I asked.

"Nothing," replied Yehuda.

"Did you try to find out?" I asked.

"At first, I was just afraid: in the 40's and 50's asking such questions was not safe. But later I tried to make inquiries but without success. No documents remained." Yehuda replied.

"That's one more righteous person, whose tracks were lost in the boundless expanse of the Stalinist gulag," I thought. Then in my thoughts I turned to that person in the name of my hero: "Dear Victor Chekanov, my savior, my friend, my adopted brother! I'm sorry I could not save you, as you once saved me. But if you're still alive, or your relatives live, know that I remember and love you as a brother, I pray for your soul to our common G-d. People

HOW MUCH FURTHER

such as you are the pride of Russia; thanks to ones like you, one day its people will live happily. I believe in it!"

Yehuda continued, "Then, of course, I went to Pochep, the city of my childhood. Arriving in town, I talked with the survivors and immediately learned that my relatives were killed and my house was burnt. I was told that in 1941, even before the arrival of the Germans in Pochep, my father was given a horse and a cart and advised to leave the city; it was already known that the Germans were annihilating Jews.

My father went in the direction of **Bryansk** and my sisters remained in the city, hoping that they would not be harmed. On the way, my father met a man in the uniform of a Red Army officer who told him, 'Why are you leaving? Go back, the Germans will not harm you.' Father believed him and went back to meet his death."

"What kind of officer was that?" I thought. "From where did he get this kind of information? Did he say it out of ignorance or on purpose? It's now too late to find out, a pity."

Bryansk – a city located about 235 miles southwest of Moscow. In 1918, the Belarusian Republic claimed the town but in 1919 it was taken by the Bolsheviks. During World War II, Bryansk was occupied by the Germans (from October 6, 1941 to September 17, 1943) and the city was heavily damaged by fighting. About 60,000 Soviet partisans were active in and around Bryansk, inflicting heavy losses on the German army.

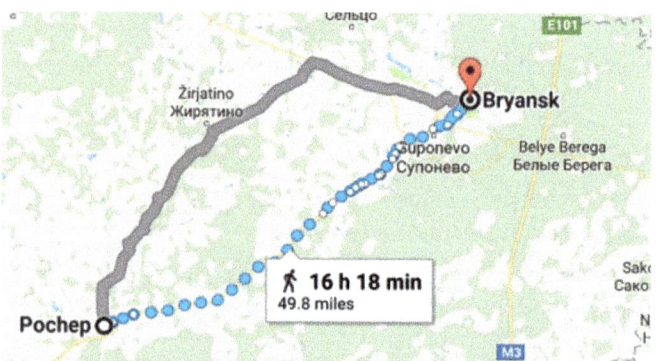

Itzhak Feldman's ill-fated walk from Pochep to Bryansk.
Map data ©2017 Google

HOW MUCH FURTHER

Yehuda continued, "As soon as the fascists occupied Pochep, they issued a decree in which all Jews and Communists were to gather in a specified place the next day at 10 in the morning. Suspecting nothing, the next morning my father first entered the building to which he was ordered to report. At the entrance stood a sentry with a band on his arm and a swastika on the band.

Ein Jude?' Asked the sentry.

My father wore a long beard, as he was religious. A German officer coming out onto the porch saw a bearded Jew and immediately called a soldier to remove the beard; but for a religious man that was like death. My father began to resist. For this the officer ordered my father to be brought to a local airfield.

Father's hands were tied, he was put on a wing of an airplane and then before takeoff the ropes were cut, leaving him holding on to the wing. After takeoff, the poor man still tried to hold on to the wing, but he soon fell to the ground, in the heart of the city."

> *Ein Jude?* –
> literally translated means "a Jew?"

Jews were required to register and wear a star, 1941.
Attribution: Bundesarchiv, Bild 101I-138-1091-11A / Kessler, Rudolf / CC-BY-SA 3.0.

HOW MUCH FURTHER

"An amusing sight for the fascists," I thought. Like a circus attraction. What kind of a monster do you have to become to stop seeing and feeling the suffering of another person and mock a defenseless old man. But then again, for a Nazi a Jew is not a person.

Our conversation continued: "When the people ran to my father's bloody corpse, the German officer said that such reprisal awaits anyone who would resist. The people looked and cried. It was the first public murder in the city.

In Pochep resided Communists and 250 Jews. All the Jews registered in the commandant's office but no one registered as a Communist. Before the arrival of the Germans the Communists and the Komsomol received secret orders from the Soviet central command to organize a guerrilla resistance squad. Upon seeing what the occupiers were doing in the city, the Communists and the Komsomol members who were unable to evacuate organized a **Soviet partisan** [guerrilla] unit and named it after my father. This detachment moved in the **Bryansk Forests**.

Soviet partisan – resistance movements that fought a guerrilla war against the Nazi forces in the Soviet Union and the occupied territories of interwar Poland in 1941 – 1945. The primary objective was the disruption of the Eastern Front's German rear, especially road and rail.

Bryansk Forests – is now a nature reserve near the Russian border with Ukraine. It is one of the last remaining unbroken forests on the southern end. The reserve covers an area of 47.05 sq. mi.

Soviet partisans on the road in Belarus, 1944.
Attribution: Author unknown; public domain.

HOW MUCH FURTHER

Unsolicited, the song **Rang aloud Bryansk Forest** sounded in my ears.

That meant in Belarus there were whole partisan groups which consisted almost entirely of Jews. Stalin's propaganda worked so well that we didn't even suspect it! '***Ivan's fighting in the trenches - Abram trades in rabkope***' was a common phrase of the time!'

Yehuda added: "All this I learned from my cousin Abram, Communist and soldier of a partisan detachment. His detachment received an order from central command from the Commissar for Defense of the Soviet Union **Timoshenko** to return to the territories seized the Germans. All the forces of the Red Army and the partisans were sent to do it."

"What was the fate of the Jews who remained in Pochep?" I asked. "After all, there were your sister with her family and your aunts were there. What happened to them?"

"They were placed in the former incubator building [of a poultry processing plant] and not allowed to eat or drink. On May 15, 1942 all of them were shot. There my sister and her children died."

Rang aloud Bryansk Forest – the video to the song can be found on YouTube: www.youtube.com/watch?v=xu2wDkO0pb8

Ivan's fighting in the trenches - Abram trades in rabkope – "Jews were not at war" was a commonplace saying. To be a Jew at the front was not safe. Their comrades, while retreating, could throw the Jews to their fate, while understanding that German captivity for a Jew meant certain death. More in Appendix 4.

Semyon Timoshenko, 1938.
Attribution: Magazine Ogonyok; public domain.

HOW MUCH FURTHER

A tense silence hung in the room. My companion added to his story: "They were shot not by Germans but by Ukrainians, who were criminals from Soviet prisons."

"Also great friends of the Communists and the fascists," I thought. "Further proof of how little the cruelty of communism differs from that of fascism."

"What about the partisans?" I asked. "Didn't they know about the impending massacre?"

"The partisans wanted to save the people but did not have time. Upon breaking into the city and seeing the bodies of those shot, they gave the Nazis a fierce battle and again disappeared into the woods."

A heavy silence fell anew. Suddenly, a soft and melodious singing sounded. Yehuda sang in Hebrew, apparently only to himself, forgetting about us and everything in the world. I did not understand all the words but felt that he was complaining to someone and asking for something.

Timoshenko – Semyon Timoshenko was a Soviet military commander who befriended Stalin. In September 1942 he was sent to Ukraine to restore order in the Southwestern Front at the gates of Kiev.

Yehuda's nephews, his sister's children, Abraham and Reyzele, killed in Pochep, May 15, 1942.

HOW MUCH FURTHER

"What was it?" I asked when he fell silent.

"It was a Kaddish, a memorial prayer for all who died in that terrible war," Yehuda answered.

"How do you know this Kaddish?" I asked.

"I wrote it myself," he said simply. He handed me a sheet with the printed Hebrew text of the prayer.

Here it is translated [and edited by Luda]:

> "Where are you, our beloved? Never will we see your graves. In memory of you I say this memorial prayer.
>
> Lord, I appeal to You! I, your saved son, Yehuda Feldman. I ask that you give those who have served you and died, a place in the Garden of Eden!
>
> And all say amen!"

We were silent.

"But when you prayed you named names. Who are they?" I asked.

"These were the names of my family members who were killed there: father, sister, aunt, nephews." He replied and repeated the names in a chant:

1. Feldman Itzhak - father
2. Feldman Genia - sister
3. Abraham and Reyzele (Rosie) - sister's children
4. Esther - cousin

HOW MUCH FURTHER

"Out of a total of 250 people who were shot, 27 were my relatives. Forgive me dear ones that my memory has already so weakened that I do not remember all of your names. But in my heart you will forever remain," Yehuda lamented.

Again, it was quiet, as if the souls of the deceased listened to the sounds of their names. It is said that the dead are alive while they are remembered. So let the souls of those whose names are mentioned in this prayer rejoice.

Cautiously I asked: "After 1945, were you ever again in Pochep?"

He shook his head sadly: "No. What would I do there? None of my relatives were left alive."

"But isn't there even a monument to the Jews shot in May 1942? After all, there are monuments even in small villages," I asked.

"I have no one to write to and ask about it," he replied.

Yet, perhaps, there still are surviving witnesses of every-thing that was going on there or their descendants. Where are you? **Answer back**!

Answer back – there are two monuments to World War II in Pochep; one for the Jews massacred and one for the fallen soldiers. More in Appendix 5.

World War II monuments in Pochep; one for the Jews massacred and one for the fallen soldiers, 2016.
Attribution: Photo by Beth Galleto (Jewish monument).
Attribution: Volodya Mozhenkov (Soldier monument).

X
FAREWELL TO KURT!

"So, you're once again captain of medical service Yehuda Feldman. As I understand it, you went to Kolomna and Pochep for personal, not official, reasons, as if on vacation. But after you returned from vacation, where you directed?" I asked.

He continued, "I was appointed Chief of the Medical Unit of the **Ryazan** Camp for German Prisoners of War.

I worked there about half a year before the evacuation of prisoners to Germany when the camp closed. Here again fate brought me together with Kurt, my bodyguard and friend who helped me so in Norway. Now our roles were reversed: he needed my help and I did everything for him to be released from captivity as soon as possible. Before his departure, we talked long and sincerely. When I told him about the death of my relatives in Pochep, his face turned ashen. He repeated that he was hurt and ashamed for Germany and its people, who allowed these atrocities against innocent people."

"Do you know anything about Kurt's fate? What was his last name? In what city did he live? Is he still alive?" I asked.

> *Ryazan* – a city located about 122 miles southeast of Moscow. Immediately after World War II, rapid development of the city began. Massive factories were constructed in the city, including the largest refinery in Europe and the Soviet Union's only producer of potato harvesting equipment: Ryazselmash Plant.

HOW MUCH FURTHER

German prisoners of war in Moscow at the end of 1944.
Attribution: RIA Novosti archive, image #129359 / Michael Trahman / CC-BY-SA 3.0.

"No, I don't know anything. Correspondence with foreign countries, especially Germany, was under the strict surveillance by the KGB. If they knew I had attempted to correspond they would never have allowed me to go to Israel, even from the **Baltic States**. And now I forgot his last name. So many years have passed!" Yehuda lamented.

"Let's try to turn to Kurt through the pages of this book. Perhaps it will get to Germany, and a person who knew Kurt will respond?" I suggested. He agreed.

> *Dear Kurt! Your behavior towards Soviet prisoners in Norway in the years 1942-45 in the Andals deserves our respect and admiration. Such as you are the conscience of the German people, their color, and pride. If not for such people as you, never would present day Germany know repentance, rebirth, or prosperity!*

Baltic States – the Baltic states of Latvia, Lithuania, and Estonia were part of the Russian Empire since the end of the 18th century, but after the Russian Revolution of 1917 they became independent states.

In 1940, the Red Army occupied the Baltic States and following rigged elections the three countries formally applied to 'join' the Soviet Union in August 1940.

Although part of the Soviet Union, the Baltic States retained their culture (though the official language became Russian), closer ties to Europe, and a desire for independence.

HOW MUCH FURTHER

XI
AFTER THE DEMOBILIZATION

"I was offered an opportunity by the military commissariat [recruitment office] to go North, but I refused," Yehuda continued.

(I did not think that a military man could refuse, but they must have suggested, not ordered).

"Then they demobilized me, the Ministry of Health sent me to the *Altai region*. There I was the head physician of the *Rebrikhinsky District* Hospital. Strictly speaking, there wasn't a hospital yet, but rather a health center with just one nurse and ten patients - no doctor. And this was for the whole district! I grew the clinic to forty beds and with the appearance of a doctor, patients began to come much

Altai region – a federal subject of Russia. The climate is severe with long, cold, dry winters and hot, usually dry summers. The region has huge reserves of raw materials, especially materials used for building, as well as significant mineral reserves.

Rebrikhinsky District – located in the North, it is one of fifty-nine districts in Altai.

Yehuda after demobilization, 1945.

HOW MUCH FURTHER

more. I also opened a maternity ward. After two years the area had a real hospital. For this work, I was awarded the Certificate of Merit by the Altai Regional Executive Committee," he added proudly.

"Three years I worked in that arctic region [Altai Region]. I was a doctor in the gold mines and treated both civilians and prisoners who worked there. From there in 1947 I went to *Yakutsk*.

Yakutsk – located about 280 miles south of the Arctic Circle. It is a major supplier of diamonds. Its average winter temperature is −30 °F (−34 °C), which makes Yakutsk the coldest city of its size or greater in the world.

From Ryazan camp for German prisoners, to head physician in the Altai region, and then to work in Yakutsk.
Map data ©2017 Google

Temperature (-48° F with wind chill) in Yakutsk in January 2018.

HOW MUCH FURTHER

He went of his own accord, not because he was assigned by the military commissariat! He was offered to go to work in the North! "But work you enjoy never feels too hard," goes the Russian proverb.

There was a real [large] clinic here and of course, a quite large and friendly staff. Here I met Miriam, my future wife.

She worked as an accountant in the clinic. How did she end up in Yakutsk? Before the war she lived with her parents in Riga in the Baltic States.

Her father [David and his wife Rivka] was a wealthy industrialist. With the arrival of the Red Army in 1940 his factory was confiscated and the **family was deported** to Yakutsk.

After our wedding we got an apartment, but soon an opportunity came up to move from the blustery Yakutsk back to the South, in the Altai Territory, to the city of **Biysk**.

There I worked as a doctor in the hospital for disabled war veterans. Here, in Biysk, our two daughters were born."

Family was deported – the Soviet doctrine of the time called for the old "bourgeois" societies to be destroyed to make room for a new socialist society, run by loyal Soviet citizens. In May 1941, NKVD secret police issued a top secret directive declaring the enemies of the Soviet state are "under arrest or subject to deportation without any legal process." On June 14, about 17,500 Lithuanians were deported. More in Appendix 6.

Biysk – in the late 19th - early 20th centuries Biysk became a large trading center of South Siberia that dealt with England, France, and Germany.

Nearly 50,000 citizens of the Baltics were sent to the gulag in 1941.
Attribution: bundesarchiv, bild 137-065360 / sigl / cc-by-sa 3.0.

HOW MUCH FURTHER

Uspenskaya St, Biysk Russia, mid 20th century.
Attribution: Author unknown; public domain.

Listening to his story, I wondered: "Not a word about the dark post-war years and hard times for the Jews!" But what would be the cost to recount these terrible disasters: the fight against "*rootless cosmopolitans*", the death of prominent Jewish figures of science and culture, mass layoffs of Jews under various pretexts, and obstacles to Jewish applicants for admission to universities.

Yes, take for example the notorious "Doctor's Case" and the subsequent flood of slander against Jewish doctors, the accusation of sabotage, and the refusal to be treated by them. This was only a small part of what had to be endured in the USSR by the long-suffering people, who had just experienced the terrible days of fascist occupation! He wasn't touched by all this at all? Again, I recall what was said by my companion: "I swear that in 51 years that I lived in the USSR (before leaving for Israel), I felt no anti-Semitism at all!"

He swore, "Could a deeply religious Jew break one of the Ten Commandments: do not bear false witness?"

> ***Rootless cosmopolitans*** – since 1948 the Soviet Union had a campaign to combat cosmopolitanism - people with connections to many different countries and cultures. The campaign acquired an anti-Semitic form in the fight against "rootless cosmopolitans", who often turned out to be people with Jewish names. There were unspoken instructions not to allow Jews to senior positions. More in Appendix 7.

HOW MUCH FURTHER

Yehuda and Miriam Feldman right after their marriage in Biysk, 1951.

At that time in the wilderness, hospitals were non-existent and every doctor was worth his weight in gold. Apparently, there Jewish doctors were not targeted. To expel the Jews who already lived there – how much further?

In the case of Yehuda it was so: in the early 1950's, he was already working in Yakutsk and then in Biysk. By local standards, this was a major center of the Urals in Eastern Siberia and the Altai Territory. There was a large peer group: in the Yakutsk clinic there was even an accountant, his future wife. His oldest daughter was born in Biysk in 1951, on the eve of the "*Doctor's Case*".

I asked Yehuda: "Were there Communist party organizations in the Yakutsk or Biysk clinics?"

"Yes, of course," he answered.

"Were there staff meetings conducted concerning 'doctor felons' or 'rootless cosmopolitans'? I asked.

"Conducted," he replied.

"And the protocols drawn up?" I asked.

"And the protocol," he answered.

> *Doctor's Case* – a criminal case against a group of prominent Soviet Jewish doctors accused of conspiracy and murder of a number of Soviet leaders. The alleged conspiracy started in 1948, when the doctor Lydia Timashuk was forced by Soviet Intelligence to write a different diagnosis for the treatment of Andrei Zhdanov. Zhdanov was a post-World War II hero who was thought to be the successor-in-waiting to Stalin, but who died before Stalin. More in Appendix 7.

HOW MUCH FURTHER

"And sent to the right place?" I asked.

"And sent," he answered.

"Did they not fire any of the Jews? Including you?" I asked.

"No, no one. I worked as head of the MCC (Medical-Control Commission); a high position which required a lot of experience and qualification. My '**Work Book**' had only gratitude. Although not a member of the [Communist] party, I was well respected. With the [SMERSH] war camp in the past, I was beyond reproach: my innocence has been fully proven."

Here I realized: always and everywhere there are the fanatics, who bring the country and the people great harm (with the best of intentions). There are also people with common sense who do not look at the questionnaire but at the man, they do not openly act out against the authorities

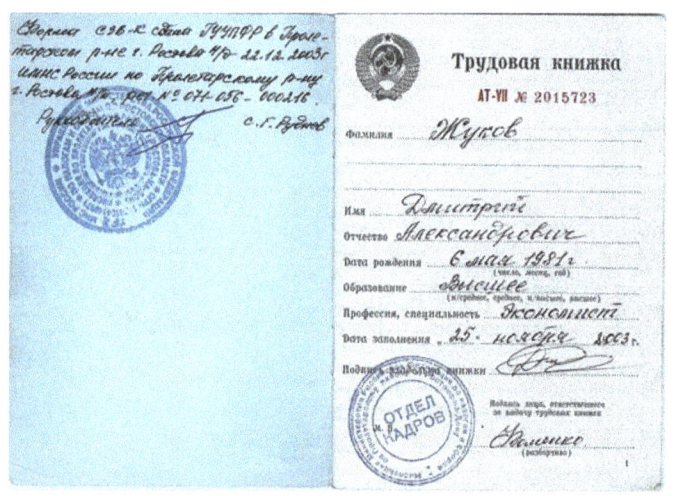

Trudovaya knizhka USSR (Work Book), 1974.
Attribution: Dmitriy Zhukov; public domain.

> **Work Book –** jobs in the Soviet Union were government controlled and workers monitored. Every worker was required to carry a passport and an official government issued Work Book.
>
> The Work Book was a worker's only official resume, but written by their managers. Notable awards, achievements, reprimands, and politically deviant behavior were all recorded.
>
> Falsifying any part of the Work Book led to arrest and being noted a Jew led to discrimination.

HOW MUCH FURTHER

but treat stupid directives "from above" purely with formality: write the correct paper for the authorities and go no further. Yehuda lucked out again. Apparently among the [Communist] party overseers there were reasonable people, not just obedient fools, who, it is known, can be more dangerous than the enemy.

> It could take months to verify a former Prisoner of War status with Moscow, so the filtration camps findings would be part of the Work Book.

XII
ISRAEL!

"I have already recounted that my wife was a native of the Baltic States," Yehuda said. "Prior to the war, her family lived in **Riga**.

In the middle of the 1950's, after the death of Stalin, my wife's parents moved back to their homeland, to Riga. In 1961 my wife and daughters also went to Riga and bought an apartment there.

Since 1964, I regularly listened to radio broadcasts from Israel. My wife's mother had a brother in Israel, they corresponded, and we received parcels. Relatives of my wife insistently invited us to **come to Israel**."

Riga – the capital and the largest city of Latvia. The Baltic States in the Soviet Union are nicknamed 'our little West' and there is more truth than irony. Crossing the border, a resident of the USSR found himself in a completely different world; a foreign country.

From Yakutsk to Biysk Siberia and finally to Riga in Latvia.
Map data ©2017 Google

HOW MUCH FURTHER

Riga, 1960.
Attribution: Author unknown; public domain.

"This, in the 1960's, was only possible in the Baltics," I thought. In the USSR in the years of the **Khrushchev's Thaw** the attitude toward the Jews was almost the same as under Stalin, but without the executions and the concentration camps: timely death for the 'leader of all the people [Stalin].' About the rest: friendship with the Arabs (headed by Nasser) and proclaiming that Zionism was a form of fascism. At that time correspondence with or going to Israel, even to visit, was not even worth talking about.

My companion continued: "The history of Jewish immigration (Aliyah) is full of tragic events. Suffice it to recall the early 1950's, when **Golda Meir,** the than Consul and future Prime Minister of Israel, arrived in Moscow.

She appealed to Stalin with a request to allow the Soviet Jews, who so desired, to repatriate to Israel. Stalin replied: 'Absolutely let them go.' The Jews were delighted and brought their applications to the Visa Office, after which they were immediately sent to the camps."

> *Come to Israel* – freedoms in the Soviet Union were limited. All parcels and correspondence in/out of the country were searched.
>
> The Jews faced open anti-Semitism but were forbidden from leaving. To request emigration, a foreign relative had to file a petition with the Soviet Consulate and pay a $1000 USD fee.
>
> After a petition the family and any relatives remaining in Russia were likely to be interviewed by the KGB and possibly jailed, and / or black listed from work. Many families ended up cutting ties before emigrating to limit reprisal from the authorities.

HOW MUCH FURTHER

Golda Meir, 1973.
Attribution: Library of Congress; public domain.

> *Khrushchev's Thaw* – a period from the early 1950's to early 1960's when repression and censorship in the Soviet Union were relaxed, and millions of Soviet political prisoners were released from Gulag labor camps due to policies of de-Stalinization and peaceful coexistence with other nations.

I remember, "You can go to Israel through **Magadan**,"

Yuliy Chersanovich Kim sang, in the middle of the 1980's. How much bitterness is in that joke!

"Upon finding out this, a perturbed Golda Meir immediately left the Soviet Union," added Yehuda.

After the "Doctor's Case," Israel completely broke off diplomatic relations with the USSR," I remember. A lot more water passed under the bridge before the [USSR] authorities in the 1970's under **Brezhnev** and in need of

> *Golda Meir* – an Israeli teacher, political leader, and the 4th Israeli Prime Minister. She was the first and only woman to hold such an office and described as the "Iron Lady" of Israeli politics.

Lenin Street, Magadan, 2008.
Attribution: Johannes Rohr; public domain.

HOW MUCH FURTHER

Yuliy Chersanovich Kim, 2006.
Attribution: Al Silonov; public domain.

Magadan – a port town located on the Sea of Okhotsk. From 1932 to 1953, it held a vast and brutal forced-labor camp and gold operation. The town later served as a port for exporting gold and other metals mined.

pipes for oil which could only be obtained from the United States, were forced to slightly open a crack and allow partial Jewish emigration.

Yehuda continued: "We in 1972 as a family left Riga to immigrate to Israel [more about the Khrushchev's Thaw later]. Our first step was from the USSR to Austria, where I was offered to stay but refused because I wanted to go to the home of my ancestors."

Yuliy Chersanovich Kim – one of Russia's foremost bards, a composer, poet, and songwriter. His songs, encompassed everything from mild humor to biting political satire appear in at least fifty Soviet movies. He immigrated to Israel in 1998.

Brezhnev in East Berlin, 1967.
Attribution: Bundesarchiv, Bild 183-F0417-0001-011 / Kohls, Ulrich / CC-BY-SA 3.0.

HOW MUCH FURTHER

Here starts the fulfillment of the prophetic dream that Yehuda saw in captivity. How commendable that he did not stay in the peaceful and prosperous Austria but went to a country whose people lived in constant danger. But it was his country and his people.

"We were supposed to fly in an airplane, which later, in flight, was hijacked by terrorists; but through successful negotiation the passengers were released. But before the [our] flight we were transferred to another plane and we flew safely, without any incidents. That's how G-d helped me and saved me from dangers! And still does this day."

> *Brezhnev* – Leonid Brezhnev was the leader of the Communist Party from 1964 until his death in 1982. His eighteen year term was second in duration only to that of Joseph Stalin.

XIII
IN ISRAEL!

"At the airport, called **Ben Gurion** we were met by the Israeli authorities. In the plane there were about 60 of us 'passengers'. Next we were sorted by profession.

We were given a taxi and driven to **Beersheva**. I was given a three-bedroom apartment and even (at first, while I studied in an **Ulpan**) free meals and 60 Lire a month. This was approximately equal to 3000 Shekels. A chicken of any weight cost 3 Lire. A bottle of the best cognac 5 Lire."

"What about work?" I asked.

"At that time good, experienced doctors were in great demand everywhere in Israel. That's why, as soon as I completed my studying at Ulpan, I was offered a job in the Dead Sea area, where at that time the **Pan-American Hotel** was being built. There, I successfully passed the examination for the title of general practitioner: correctly diagnosed a patient and prescribed treatment at the Soroka Hospital. Immediately afterwards I was assigned to one of the clinics in the position of family doctor."

"And here in 1973 you were caught by the **Yom Kippur War**?" I asked.

"Yes. I remember that day well. On Yom Kippur I was in the synagogue. A woman ran in and yelled: 'The war has begun!' Two countries had attacked us: Syria and Egypt.

Ben Gurion – Israel's main international airport and by far the busiest airport in the country.

Beersheva – the largest city in the Negev desert of southern Israel.

Ulpan – a school designed for the intensive study of Hebrew to teach adult immigrants the basic language skills.

Pan-American Hotel – now the Moriah Plaza Hotel Eilat.

HOW MUCH FURTHER

Back then the Israeli Prime Minister was Golda Meir and Defense Minister was Moshe Dayan. Golda Meir wanted to use nuclear weapons, but Moshe Dayan did not allow it. We would have reached Cairo, if not for the intervention of the United States.

"And the USSR," I add mentally.

Aloud, I asked: "What did you do during the Yom Kippur War?"

"I already worked as a senior physician at one of the low rent districts (do not remember its name). Back then the coast of the Dead Sea was a huge construction site," he replied.

"And were the wounded taken there?" I asked.

"No, the wounded had assigned hospitals," he responded.

"What changed in the country during the war? Did you feel that there was a war?" I asked.

"Of course. Missiles flew at Israel, but G-d saved the country, and the rockets fell into the sea," he responded.

I was reminded of the proverb: "G-d helps those who help themselves." More often should the country's leaders remember this wisdom! Then they would not have blundered into the **Second Lebanon** [War]. But what will happen no one knows. In a word, "if you want peace - prepare for war."

My companion continued: "After the Yom Kippur War, I had to change where I worked many times, until settling in **Herzliya**. Here I bought an apartment in which I live to this day. In 1986, I retired. But more recently, Germany began to pay me a pension as a former concentration camp prisoner. I live well and do not

---

Yom Kippur War – fought and lost by a coalition of Arab states led by Egypt and Syria against Israel from October 6 to 25, 1973.

Second Lebanon War – a month long conflict between Israeli and Hezbollah forces in Lebanon during the summer of 2006.

Herzliya – an affluent city in the central coast of Israel; known for its robust start-up and entrepreneurial culture.

HOW MUCH FURTHER

Sokolov St, Herzliya, 2008.
Attribution: Mar Garina; public domain.

complain. Children and grandchildren are grown up. There is even a great grandchild."

"But here you have lived through another two more major wars: The first **Lebanon War** (1982) and the **Gulf War** (1991)." I continued.

"In the city of Herzliya, where I lived, the wars were not felt. Of course, war is war, and does not happen without its causalities. But in general, the city lived calmly." He explained.

"As in the Second Lebanon [War] last August," I thought. The center of our small country is still reliably protected from enemy missiles. But will it always be this way? Anyway, since moving to Herzliya my hero and his family, need not fear for their lives. In case of war, of course, there are no guarantees.

"You did not say anything about the fate of your brother and his family, or the fate of the husband of your sister," I reminded him.

Lebanon War – lasted from June to September 1982 when the Israel Defense Forces entered southern Lebanon, after repeated attacks and counter-attacks from the Palestine Liberation Organization (PLO) operating in southern Lebanon.

Gulf War – fought from August 2, 1990 to February 28, 1991, starting with the buildup of troops and defense of Saudi Arabia. It was a war waged by coalition forces from 35 nations led by the United States against Iraq in response to Iraq's invasion and annexation of Kuwait.

HOW MUCH FURTHER

"Brother Geya Itzhakovich at the end of trade school entered the Moscow Pedagogical Institute named after **Bubnov**, from which he graduated in 1937. Later he went to the front lines and was killed in Moscow in 1942. His son, my nephew, is still alive. My sister and her children, as I have said, died in Pochep during the occupation. Her husband, drafted to the front, was an attendant to a KGB general and survived. He, with a new wife and daughter, moved to Israel. The parents have already died, but the daughter is alive."

Andrei Bubnov, 1920's or 1930's.
Attribution: Author unknown; public domain.

Bubnov –
Andrei Bubnov was a Bolshevik revolutionary leader in Russia. Bubnov was born to a Russian merchant family and studied at the Moscow Agricultural Institute where as a student he joined the Russian Social Democratic Labor Party in 1903. He was expelled from the Moscow University for revolutionary activities.

In 1929, he became the Commissar for Education, ended the period experimental educational, and switched the emphasis to practical industrial skills.

He was arrested by the secret police in 1937 and shot soon after.

HOW MUCH FURTHER

XIV
MY COUNTRY ISRAEL!

In conclusion, I could not resist asking questions about his impressions of Israel, about the arrival of which he dreamed at the most terrible moments of his life.

"How was it to live in Israel during the 1970's, what was it like at the time you came here?" I asked.

"At that time, the Prime Minister was Golda Meir. Israel then lived very well: G-d willing my children, grandchildren, and great-grandchildren to live not worse. Judge for yourself: working as a family doctor, I earned 1840 Lire. In the USSR, not even a professor dared to dream of such money. Most of my patients had cars. There was no problem with food. To every arriving specialist (if their profession was necessary for the country) a personal consultant was assigned, who tracked the employment of his ward after completing Ulpan. Immediately after getting a job, a specialist received government sponsored housing; a three-room apartment with appliances. A year later they bought-out the housing at an affordable price. After **currency reform**, the apartments became even cheaper."

"Tell us about Herzliya in the 1970's," I requested.

"The city was gradually built. Take, for example, one of the central streets – street of Ha'atzmaut (Independence). In its place was sand and now - look at the houses!

HOW MUCH FURTHER

On January 1, 1986 the new shekel replaced the old shekel, at a rate of 1,000 old to 1 new.

Attribution: Bank of Israel; used within copyrighted restrictions.

Previously, when it rained, water rose to the knee, it was impossible to cross the street. And now - asphalt, traffic lights. A modern city, flourishing, beautiful, and green! It grew before my eyes.

As for supplying the city with groceries, by the time of my arrival the store shelves were bursting with food, customers were allowed to sample the products they were going to buy. Goods were exhibited on tables and if you would try a little of everything, you could eat until you burst."

"But it was not always like this," I said. "I read Golda Meir's memoir 'My Life'. In the forties and fifties Israel was a hungry and a scary place to live. How did the country manage to end this and achieve prosperity?"

After thinking, he answered: "The people in power, led by Golda Meir, were simple and modest people in their daily lives. For this, the [Israeli] people loved them, and they loved their people. Golda Meir traveled all over the world, telling about a young Jewish state, called for help to get it on its feet. And people all over the world (first and foremost Jews) helped how they could: both materially and morally. Respect for Israel and its leaders was very high."

"You cannot say that about the current leaders," I thought.

Currency reform – in the years after the 1973 Yom Kippur War, Israel's growth stalled, inflation soared, and government expenditures rose. Then, in 1983, Israel suffered "the Bank stock crisis". By 1984 inflation reached an annual rate close to 450% and projected to reach over 1000% by the end of the following year. In response, the 1985 Economic Stabilization Plan introduced steps including significant cuts to government spending and the devaluation of the Shekel. On January 1, 1986 the new Shekel replaced the old Shekel, at a rate of 1,000 old to 1 new.

HOW MUCH FURTHER

Herzliya in 1964 and in 2008.
Attribution: Cohen Fritz; public domain.
Attribution: Shimon Shwai; public domain.

Yehuda again (for the umpteenth time!), as if guessing my thoughts, said: "Our current leaders could learn from the country's first leaders about modesty."

"Woe to the people who do not have a real leader!" He proclaimed in a stern voice."

But why did Israel, after winning so many wars, lose so much territory?" I asked.

He answered: "In the Holy Book it is written, 'What G-d gives, you cannot give away to anyone. And what did the Jews do? Gave Egypt Sinai.'"

"At the very time of almost reaching Cairo!" I remembered.

Yehuda continued, "This was a country built on donations."

"But after all, the country was headed, as a rule, by military generals, who fought for her and defeated her enemies. Why, then, did the country win nothing from the victories won by them?"

"You mean **Rabin, Barak, and Sharon**?" He asked and answered: "They were brave warriors, but were incapable of leading the country."

Rabin, Barak, and Sharon – former Prime Ministers of Israel.

"But the present day's leaders' military past does not even shine!" I added bitterly. "Why did we choose them?"

"Who chose them?" He answered my question with a question. "We do not know for whom we vote."

"New leaders are needed and new ideas," I said. "But it's not up to us to do. May G-d send young and fresh leadership, as it is said, '*poured new wine into old wineskins*.'"

"G-d willing," repeated Yehuda, "Then Israel will live and prosper."

> ***Poured new wine into old wineskins*** – parable found in the New Testament.

APPENDIX I
SPRING LOVE (LYUBOV YAROVAYA)

For some background this was been based on Wikipedia: https://ru.wikipedia.org/wiki/Любовь_Яровая_(спектакль,_1951)

Lyubov Yarovaya was a 1926 play by Konstantin Trenyov. In 1953 Lyubov Yarovaya was adapted as a Soviet drama film.

The action takes place during the Russian Civil War; 1917 - 1922. In a small town occupied by the Red Army in Crimea (Ukraine); the local authority is headed by Commissioner Roman Koshkin, a man hard enough, but trusting. Around him, a lot of people who secretly hated the Bolsheviks.

A small southern town keeps changing hands. The teacher Lyubov Yarovaya is helping the underground revolutionaries. Unexpectedly, she meets her husband, Lieutenant Yarovoy, deemed killed in World War I (1914 – 1918), who has been secretly helping the other side.

Lyubov Yarovaya staged at the Chechen Oblast Drama Theatre, 1901.
Attribution: N.L Odincov; public domain.

APPENDIX II
CHILDREN VANYUSHINA

Written by Sergey Naydyonov, a Russian playwright, the play shows the collapse of a merchant's family. The head of the family turns out to be a stranger to his children. Sharp contradictions, malice, antagonism, and greed rule the family.

The main character of the play, Vanyushin - the father of a large family, is the Russian King Lear. Both parents open their eyes to their own children only in their old age. The children, living side by side with their parents but unbeknownst to them, have grown indifferent, materialistic, and egoistic.

Vanyushin bitterly reaps the fruits of his omission as a parent and a teacher, and still hopes to reach out to his children, to distract them from the worship of material things, to sow in their souls the rational, the good, the eternal. But it is late, time has been lost and there is nowhere to sow. Terrible dreams, the phantoms of Vanyushina, turn into reality. Unable to find a way out of this situation, he commits suicide.

Children Vanyushina, staged at the private theater of Fedor Korsh in Moscow, 1901.
Attribution: Cohen Fritz; public domain.

APPENDIX III
DEMBLINSK FORTRESS

A fortress in Poland also known as Ivangorod Fortress. For some background this was been based on: http://starcom68.livejournal.com/955698.html

Demblinsk Fortress / Ivangorod Fortress, 2013.
Attribution: Author unknown; public domain.

From autumn of 1941 until February 1944 Demblinskoy fortress (the citadel and several neighboring forts) operated as German Stalag 307, through which passed about 150,000 Soviet prisoners of war. More than half of them died from hunger, cold, disease (especially in the winter of 1941-1942, when up to 500 people were killed per day), or because security guards shot prisoners for any reason and even for fun. At the time 120,000 prisoners remained in the camp. Conditions of detention were inhuman; many prisoners were placed in the open air on the parade ground of the camp. Conditions in the barracks, with bare stone floors, were only slightly better. Almost the only food served was bread made from wood flour, milled straw and grass (this flour was called Pell-mell).

What grass grew in the camp, the prisoners simply ate. Cases of cannibalism were documented. When some of the sick and the wounded were transferred to nearby Fort Balonna, considered a hospital, the prisoners did not return from it. They were given deadly injections and buried nearby in mass graves. The dead were buried in several places along fortress walls, as well as in a military cemetery a mile from the citadel.

Shortly after the war, Soviet military graves in Poland were investigated by specially created commissions, conducting selective exhumations and estimating the number of dead. That statement of the official conclusion (taken from the Polish Interia.pl site: http://facet.interia.pl/obyczaje/historia/news-stalag-307-twierdza-zaglady,nId,451287):

> "From 16 to October 21, 1947 The Polish State Commission and the Soviet Special Commission carried out an investigation of crimes committed by the Germans against Soviet POWs from Stalag 307. Based on the testimony of witnesses and the results of Soviet forensic examination it was established that 120,000-150,000 prisoners of war had passed through the camp. Due to the famine, cold, lack of basic sanitary conditions, epidemics, inhumane abuse and shooting at Stalag 307 in 1941-1942, about 80,000 prisoners of war were killed."

APPENDIX IV
IVAN'S FIGHTING IN THE TRENCHES

For some background this was been based on: http://berezin-fb.su/2014/02/817 колонка-иона-дегена-18-евреи-не-воевал/

"Jews were not at war" was a commonplace Soviet propaganda saying during WWII. To illustrate the situation, a quote from a poem by Boris Slutsky:

Boris Slutsky, 1941.
Attribution:
www.jewmil.com/biografii/item/835-slutskij-boris-abramovich.

Jews are dashing people,
They are bad soldiers:
Ivan is fighting in the trenches, Abram trades in the factory… Not having traded even once, Not stealing even once, A carry myself, like an infection, This particular race. And the bullet passes me, So they say not true:
"Jews were not killed! Everyone is back alive!"

There were Jews who had their nationality at the frontlines concealed. To be a Jew at the frontline was not safe. While retreating, their fellow soldiers could throw the Jews to their fate, while understanding that German captivity for a Jew meant certain death. Nazi guards usually ordered a column of prisoners: "Jews and Communists – come forward." If other prisoners did not know which of the captured soldiers was Jewish, it reduced the risk of someone betraying a Jew to the Nazis.

APPENDIX V
POCHEP MONUMENTS

There are two monuments to World War II in Pochep.

The Red Army liberated Pochep on September 21, 1943. According to Yad Vashem, after the liberation, in order to prevent vandalism, the Soviet authorities ordered the ditches, where the Jews were murdered, to be covered with earth. A small monument was erected at the site, but the upper part of it was stolen. In the 1960's a new monument was constructed.

Shoah Monument, 2016.
Photo by Beth Galleto.

Shoah Monument close-up, 2016.
Photo by Beth Galleto.

The Hebrew inscription reads: "A memorial to our Jewish brothers, 1,846 inhabitants of Pochep, who were brutally murdered and buried alive by the accursed Hitler's fascists on 16-17 [sic] of Adar 5702." The Russian inscription says:

"Here are buried 1,846 people brutally murdered by the fascist henchmen on March 16-17, 1942."

The second monument, dedicated to all the soldiers of WW II, is located in October Square:

Soldier monument.
Attribution: Geni Project by Volodya Mozhenkov, 2016.

APPENDIX VI
FAMILY WAS DEPORTED

The Jews of Eastern Europe have a saying, "you can only take along [when you leave] a piece of gold and your education". These words were said, throughout the years, by three generations of my family. Back to my great grandfather, David, whose family's story we will briefly touch here.

At the turn of 20th century David and Rivka were among the many Jews who lived in Kaunas (Kovno), the second largest city in Lithuania. The city was thriving, but the two young adults were very poor. They were married in 1914 and worked hard to support their family. Rivka went from house to house looking for work as a seamstress. My grandmother Miriam (Rivka's daughter who married Yehuda) told us that she and her sister Basia used to come home and wait for hours, for their parents, by the locked door on the steps on their home.

David was a dynamic man and always busy with work. He finished accounting classes, courses to become a hypnotist, and tried different kinds of businesses. He lived for a long time in Moscow, wrote his own music, and sang like an angel. When Miriam practiced piano, David from a different room would call out any mistakes she made. Miriam remembered, once a major Moscow theatre, which belonged to the Czar, offered her father a prestigious residency but only if he gave up Judaism; he refused. Even though he would have gotten a large sum of money and his family would finally be rich.

David, Miriam's father and Yehuda's father-in-law , 1950s.

Kaunas, Lithuania, 1900's
Attribution: Unknown author; public domain.

In the 1930's, David and his brother (a self-taught engineer) were sheet metal workers at a factory. The family moved to Riga, the capital of Latvia, and rented a small rundown barn. They bought sheet metal and manufactured pales. Sold one pale and bought two more sheets of metal. The brothers soon bought a machine and hired a worker; that's how their small workshop started. From there, they grew the business into a large zipper factory.

Around 1933 David traveled a lot and lived for some time in Berlin. He came back with warning of the dangerous rise of fascism in Germany. His warning fell on deaf ears; the First World War was over, the German's crushed, and in 1938 the world renowned Time magazine named Hitler "Man of the Year".

The brothers invented a special metal working process for lining metal cans; the new cans preserved their contents for much longer. In 1939 David received a gold medal from the National Exhibitions in Zurich (a global showcase held in Switzerland for Swiss arts, architecture, and the latest commercial products) for the innovation.

The factory was so successful that a group of competing factory owners from Riga approached David and offered: "name your price and get out of here, so we don't have to deal with you anymore". He was paid an "outrageous sum" and the family moved to Lithuania, Kaunus.

Between 1939 and 1940 the family opened and operated a printing factory. Advertisements were placed in local papers:

Lithuanian newspaper article advertising the Luna Factory (left Lithuanian / right German), 1940.

The advertisement read:

> Sheet metal packaging factory and sheet metal printing.
>
> Preparing different cans for: fish, meat and vegetable preserves, confectionery, cocoa, tobacco. Lacquer, colors, shoe polish, oil, pharmacy etc. As well as printed sheets.

On a large tin sheet an artist drew with special paints. These sheets were placed in a cradle and baked in a large oven. Then a cutting machine cut the tin as needed for lollipops, shoe polish, and various canned goods.

Tin from Russian shoe polish, 1920's – 1940's.
Attribution: Unknown author; public domain.

In June 1940, the Russians invaded Lithuania. The Soviet doctrine of the time called for the old "bourgeois" societies to be destroyed, so that a new socialist society, run by loyal Soviet citizens, could be constructed in their place. To the Bolsheviks, an entrepreneur, a Jew, or a business owner was a traitor to the people.

The Soviet authorities installed a Commissar (a political officer of the Communist Party), as an overseer, in the factory. David taught him everything about the factory. A year later on June 14, 1941 approximately 17,500 Lithuanians were deported. They walked into David's house, without notice, and marched the family (those in the house at the time) out with whatever they had in their hands and nothing more. The family was left with virtually nothing, but was saved from the Nazi occupation.

In a letter Miriam wrote, "A year later we were sent to the far to Siberia. On the way the war (World War II) caught up to us. There he [David] worked in the coal mines, worked in a processing plant, and worked at a construction site." The men were separated out and sent to the gulag (labor camps) to clear the vast Siberian forests. The women were sent to another part of Siberia. Miriam was forced to stand in rubber boots in knee deep frozen water and pull coal with her bare hands. Miriam's uncle sent parcels from overseas with gold watches to try to help; most arrived empty. The few that got through were used as gifts to bribe officials and ensure the family had food. After World War II, the family was able to secure permission to move to Yakutsk where they were reunited.

The origins of the deportation stem from the Molotov-Ribbentrop pact of 1939. The pact enabled Germany to invade Poland and allowed the Soviet state to establish a sphere of influence across Latvia, Lithuania, and Estonia. The Soviets began to usurp the Baltic States in 1940. A movement led by Stalin's close associates and local communists forced the presidents and governments of all three countries to resign. Rigged elections followed that installed the provisional "People's Governments".

Immediately after the elections, in May 1941, the NKVD (secret police) began the arrest deportation of "hostile elements" and members of their families. The NKVD issued a top secret directive declaring the enemies of the Soviet state are "under arrest or subject to deportation without any legal process."

The instructions emphasized that the deportations should be carried out as stealthily as possible to minimize panic and resistance. Each four-member "executive group" was given the task of deporting two families. The official instructions were for to allow each family 1 hour to take up to 100 kilograms (220 lb.) of food, clothes, shoes, and other necessities but witnesses testified that these instructions were often not followed. Many families were given less than hour to pack a suitcase and go; most left unprepared for the journey or the life at the gulag. If someone attempted to resist or run away, they would be shot or beaten. Often families would be separated and there were cases when parents, children, or spouses voluntarily reported to the train station to be deported with their captured relatives. The journey often lasted weeks if not months.

The deportations in the Baltics were interrupted by the German invasion of the Soviet Union. Nazi propaganda from that time claimed that the German forces were fighting to free the Baltic people from Soviet oppression. In June 1941, Lithuania, Hungary, and Romania all saw anti-Soviet uprisings. However, no sooner had the Soviets been expelled than the Nazis took over, replacing one brutal regime with another.

APPENDIX VII
DOCTOR'S CASE / ROOTLESS COSMOPOLITANISM

The following was been based on the Russian Wikipedia (version January 2017): https://ru.wikipedia.org/w/index.php title=Дело_врачей&oldid=83025350. For additional English based background refer to: http://www.yivoencyclopedia.org/article.aspx/Doctors_Plot.

The Doctors Case was the culmination of the policy pursued by the Soviet Union in Stalin's time. Since 1948 the Soviet Union had a campaign to combat cosmopolitanism [people with connections to many different countries and cultures], which acquired an anti-Semitic form, as so-called "rootless cosmopolitans" often turned out to be people with Jewish names. There were unspoken instructions not to allow Jews to senior positions.

In the countries of Eastern Europe, a series of political trials took place, in addition to the usual accusations of "betrayal" and plans for the "restoration of capitalism," a new "Zionism" accusation was added. In November 1952, at the trial in Czechoslovakia, 13 defendants were accused (11 of them Jews); including the General Secretary of the Central Committee of the Communist Party of the Czech Republic, Rudolf Slansky. The defendants were accused of attempting to assassinate the President of the Republic and the Chairman of the Communist Party, K. Gottwald, with the help of "doctors from the hostile camps."

Doctor's Case, or the poisoner-doctors, the investigation of Zionist conspiracy in the Soviet Ministry of State Security - a criminal case against a group of prominent Soviet doctors accused of conspiracy and murder of a number of Soviet leaders. The origins of the campaign relate to 1948, when the doctor Lydia Timashuk diagnosed Zhdanov [a Soviet politician who, after World War II, was thought to be the successor-in-waiting to Stalin - but who died before Stalin], with myocardial infarction, based on electrocardiogram. But Soviet leadership forced Lechsanupra to write a different diagnosis and treatment, contraindicated in heart attack, which led to the death of the patient.

The text of the official announcement of the arrest was issued in January 1953. It was announced that "the majority of participants in the terrorist group (Vovsi MS, BB Kogan, AI Feldman, AM Greenstein, Etinger Ya G. and others) have been linked to the international Jewish bourgeoisie-nationalist organization "Joint," created by the American intelligence service, ostensibly to provide material aid to Jews in other countries." In connection with this organization others had previously been charged and tried in the case of the Jewish Anti-Fascist Committee. Publication of the case in places acquired an anti-Semitic character and merged into a more general campaign to "fight against rootless cosmopolitanism," held in the USSR in 1947 - 1953.

The hero who exposed the murderers in white coats (popular propaganda stamp of the campaign), was Lydia Timashuk - doctor, who contacted the Central Committee with complaints of improper treatment of Zhdanov back in 1948. For help in "exposing the thrice damned killer doctors," she was awarded the Order of Lenin. The medal was canceled shortly after the death of Stalin.

The arrest of Jewish doctors spread across the USSR and ended after Stalin's death at the beginning of March 1953. On April 3 of the same year, all those arrested in the "Doctor's Case" were released and reinstated as fully rehabilitated.

www.ingramcontent.com/pod-product-compliance
Lightning Source LLC
Chambersburg PA
CBHW051552010526
44118CB00022B/2670